Local management of sc

The Education Reform Act of 1988 is the most significant piece of educational legislation in Britain since the 1944 Act. Local management of schools is a key issue, with the provisions of the Act now requiring schools to undertake specialist functions, such as budgeting and marketing, never before tackled at the institutional level.

Local Management of Schools is a positive response to the management challenges of the Education Reform Act. It explores the practical issues associated with planning and implementing new functions devolved to school level. Stressing the need for the whole school to meet the challenge, it will enable schools to focus on the implications of the Act and the issues it presents. Each chapter, written by an acknowledged expert in the field, looks at a different aspect, including:

- resource management
- financial management and budgetary preparation
- the uses of information technology
- marketing and the school
- the legal context
- personnel management and staff selection
- time management and priority setting

A clear thinking sympathetic discussion of the urgent practical issues now facing all schools, *Local Management of Schools* will be essential reading for those involved in educational management, whether teachers, governors, or administrators.

The Editors

Ernie Cave is Director of the Education Management Unit, at the University of Ulster, Jordanstown, where *Cyril Wilkinson* is Senior Lecturer.

Educational management series
Edited by Cyril Poster

Local management of schools
Some practical issues

Edited by
Ernie Cave
and

Cyril Wilkinson

First published 1990
by Routledge
11 New Fetter Lane, London EC4P 4EE

© 1990 Ernie Cave and Cyril Wilkinson

Typeset by LaserScript Limited, Mitcham, Surrey
Printed in Great Britain by Mackays of Chatham, Kent

British Library Cataloguing in Publication Data

Local management of schools: some practical issues. –
  (Educational management series)
  1. Schools management
  I. Cave, Ernie II. Wilkinson, Cyril III. Series
  371.2

0-415-04723-4
0-415-04998-9 (Pb)

Contents

Contributors

Ernie Cave is Director of the Education Management Unit of the University of Ulster. His experience covers primary, secondary, and teacher education sectors, and he was a secondary school headteacher for twenty-one years. He is co-author of *Teaching and Managing: Inseparable Activities in Schools*, Croom Helm, 1987.

Cyril Wilkinson is a Senior Lecturer in Education Management in the Faculty of Education of the University of Ulster, with particular responsibility for the M.Sc. degree in Education Management. He has been closely involved in the pioneering of education management courses and provision from the early 1970s. He is co-author of *Teaching and Managing: Inseparable Activities in Schools*, Croom Helm, 1987.

Michael Strain is a Senior Lecturer in Education Management in the Department of Further and Vocational Education of the University of Ulster. His research interests are in educational policy making, resource management, and decision making.

Dave Demick is Senior Course Tutor for the Postgraduate Diploma in Marketing in the Faculty of Business and Management. He joined the University of Ulster after twenty years' marketing experience in commerce. His current research interests include marketing in education.

Gareth Parry is a Lecturer in Educational Administration at the Coleraine campus of the University of Ulster. His research interests include teachers and the law, and teacher appraisal.

Richard Mapstone is a Senior Lecturer in Manpower Studies in the Department of Applied Economics and Human Resource Management of the University of Ulster. He worked previously at the Trades Union Congress and also the Commission on Industrial Relations. He has written extensively on the labour relations field and has chaired numerous arbitration panels and committees of enquiry.

Denise McAlister is a Senior Lecturer in Public Finance in the Faculty of Business and Management of the University of Ulster. Previously she was an HM Inspector of Taxes for the Inland Revenue. Her research interests and publications cover the areas of budgetary control, performance measurement, and public expenditure.

Michael Connolly is Professor and Head of Department of Public Administration and Legal Studies of the University of Ulster. He is joint editor of *Public Management* and includes education among his wide-ranging research interests.

Reg North is Lecturer in Education Management at the Magee College campus of the University of Ulster. He is currently engaged in managing a research project funded by the Microelectronics Education Support Unit designed to produce management training materials for information technology development within schools.

Foreword

The Education Reform Act of 1988 is quite the most significant piece of educational legislation since the 1944 Act and, because of the speed with which it is required to be implemented, may well prove to have even greater impact on the teaching profession and the public alike.

Local management of schools is the key issue, already being translated by regulations from a concept into a reality. There are, not surprisingly, a number of excellent books already in print on the subject and there will undoubtedly be yet more. Most of them are extensive texts, some of them are ardent polemics. This book is neither. It is a collection of essays by acknowledged experts in the field on which they have written, all from an institution which is rapidly making a name for itself, nationally and internationally, in the field of administration and management. Each is a commentary on one aspect of the main topic, though inevitably there is a common thread running through them all. Each, while not shying away from the issues that arise from the new requirements on educational management, has as its main focus the reality of the situation, that the Act is on the statute books and must now be made to work.

The book has been written for headteachers and senior managers in primary and secondary schools; for governors, whose responsibilities for monitoring and decision-making are far greater than is as yet commonly appreciated; and for LEA administrators and advisers, whose support for schools is going to be more important than ever before. Like the editors' own volume, *Teaching and Managing: Inseparable Activities in Schools*, this is a valuable contribution to the Routledge Education Management series.

Cyril Poster

Preface

A consequence of the Education Reform Act 1988 is that schools will be required to undertake specialist functions such as financial management, marketing, and personnel management, not normally performed in the past at institutional level in education. While it is inevitable that ultimate accountability for the exercise of these functions will rest with headteachers, they do not have to become specialists in all these areas. Tasks may be delegated and those who are required to carry them out will need training in order to acquire the necessary knowledge and competence. The headteacher's task will be to create a culture which enables the school to respond effectively to new conditions. The immediate need is for schools to focus on the implications of the Act and the issues it will present to headteachers and school managers.

This book provides an introduction to some of these issues. All the contributors are associated with the Education Management Unit of the University of Ulster, which is supported by the Faculty of Business and Management, the Faculty of Education, the Institute of Informatics and the Faculty of Social and Health Sciences.

Chapter one

The changing managerial arena

Ernie Cave

Despite considerable professional apprehension and widespread opposition, the Education Reform Act 1988 has become law and provides the framework within which schools must now operate. The Act is arguably the most radical and certainly the most comprehensive attempt ever to redesign the education system for England and Wales. Parallel legislation has been introduced for Scotland and for Northern Ireland. The Act will succeed in its ambition to reform the system, in the sense of reshaping it, by introducing extensive restructuring. Whether or not it will succeed in its declared ambition to reform the system, in the sense of making it better by the removal of existing imperfections, remains to be seen. In introducing the Bill, the Secretary of State for Education claimed to see it as a means through which standards in education would be raised. What constitutes standards is not explicitly defined but is implicit in that they are to be measured by an arguably narrow range of academic achievement and by examination success.

The means by which standards are to be raised are clear: it is to be achieved by restricting professional autonomy, by increasing parental power, by exposing the system to the forces of open market competition and by streamlining the governance of schools through curtailing the role of the local authority middle tier and greatly increasing the powers vested in the Secretary of State for Education, with the assumption of 415 new powers many of which relate directly to schools. The raising of standards is to be made visible through the system of pupil testing at the ages of 7, 11, 14, and 16. No convincing analysis has been made to support an argument that all these means will end in higher standards. The real fear is that while there may be some advantage for a minority of parents and pupils, the new provisions will certainly not result in the greatest good for the greatest number. The pessimistic view is that schools now struggle for survival in an arena not of their choosing, under rules which they find professionally disagreeable, and for prizes which they do not value.

Implications for schools

The national curriculum

There is no doubt that the Education Reform Act will have considerable impact on schools. Professional autonomy in determining the curriculum will be diminished by the introduction of a national curriculum, the provisions for which are seen by the government as the cornerstone of the programme to raise standards. All children are to receive a 'balanced and relevant' curriculum in mathematics, sciences, English, history, geography, technology, music, art, and physical education, and children of 11 to 16 are to study a foreign language. Parents will be given results of the assessments at 7, 11, 14, and 16 for their own children and aggregated results for schools so that comparisons may be made. The truth, of course, is that the curriculum a child actually receives is determined by what happens in the classroom within the general ethos and relationships of the school as an organization. Education is essentially a process the outcomes of which are difficult to measure. The belief that better education can be provided through centrally prescribed programmes of study assumes unrealistic levels of monitoring and control over what happens in classrooms.

The intentions of the national curriculum are praiseworthy but will only be realized if the professional educator is a willing partner in its delivery.

Open enrolment

The Act provides that parents will be able to enrol their child at any school that has the physical capacity (initially based on the 1979 admission number) to accept them provided that it is appropriate for the age and aptitude of the child. Open enrolments will apply in secondary schools for the 1990 intake. The assumption behind this legislation is that the operation of open-market competition for pupils will ensure that good schools will flourish and bad schools will be forced out of the market. No logical analysis or substantive evidence is presented to support such a view. The equation of freedom of choice and quality assurance may not be as valid as the Act assumes. There is little certainty about the criteria which parents may use in selecting a school. Research by Elliott (1981) provides some indication of possible factors, for example, good management, which may have influenced parents in a particular area to choose a particular school. The study is far from conclusive, however, in that it is dangerous to generalize from the choices of parents 'many of whom occupy managerial roles in local industry'. Elliott also admits that he suspects 'some parents responded in terms of the choice pattern they felt ought to, rather than did, obtain.'

There is no evidence that schools which already have been forced to close or amalgamate are *bad* schools or that schools which are over-subscribed are *good* schools. Many schools which have closed have been those serving small rural communities, those in large housing estates suffering from an ageing and immobile population, or those in run-down inner-city areas. Such schools are vulnerable to the movement of a quite small minority of pupils, and parents who wish to continue to send their children to a particular school are deprived of that choice if it closes.

There is a danger that schools facing falling enrolments because of environmental factors become caught in a downward spiral of decline over which they have no control. There are other real dangers. Parents may exercise their right of choice for social rather than educational reasons and refuse to send their children to schools that have large numbers of socially or economically deprived pupils, thus reinforcing social divisions. Similarly, schools with large numbers of ethnic-minority pupils may be unpopular with some white parents, thus creating racial segregation. Pring sets out a valid argument:

> The inappropriateness of the market metaphor needs to be exposed. It is a dangerously misleading analogy for understanding educational processes and for directing educational policies. All children matter, not just those whose parents have learnt to play the market effectively. And the improvement of schools requires long-term planning – not a quick alteration of a commodity to meet changing fashions. Furthermore, the stress upon individualism – upon individual preference – at the expense of social responsibility and cohesiveness must be a matter of concern as we become ever more closely interdependent rather than less so.
>
> (Pring 1988:96)

Parent power

The government's commitment to increasing parent power in education is central to the new legislation. Introducing the second reading of the Education Reform Bill, the Secretary of State for Education declared:

> We must give consumers of education a central position in decision making. That means freeing schools and colleges to deliver standards that parents and employers want. It means encouraging the customer to expect and demand that all education bodies do the best job possible. In a word, it means choice.
>
> (Hansard 1987 vol.123:77)

3

The notion of parents shaping educational provision is a considerable extension of previously held views on parental involvement in schools.

The desire for increased parent power may not be as widespread as the Act assumes. A clearer understanding is required of the kind of involvement parents desire and of the conditions necessary to make such involvement productive. It is accepted that parents in general are interested in their children's education and that they wish to be informed about their progress and prospects. Parent governors have usually been the most active and supportive among the members of the school's governing body. But it is the experience of many schools that parents have no wish to interfere in professional matters relating to the organization and management of internal affairs.

The emerging evidence suggests that they are more interested in outcomes than in processes. While there have been a few politically motivated parents who have seized the opportunity to exercise the new powers available to them, there has scarcely been a rush by parents to put themselves forward for election to governing bodies. Rather the contrary. The new governing bodies represent the core of continuing government policy to establish greater parent power. *The Times Educational Supplement* reported the results of their survey of sixty-one primary and secondary schools which took part in parent governor elections under the requirements of the 1986 Education Act, and concluded:

> Parents in many of the country's schools have failed to take part in Mr. Kenneth Baker's parent power revolution. In more than one in three schools which took part in Britain's biggest ever round of parent-governor elections, the turnout was less than 25 per cent. And in more than four out of ten schools, no elections were held because not enough parents were prepared to stand.
>
> (TES 21 October 1988)

The proposals for local management of schools place new and perhaps intimidating responsibilities on school governors. Although technically the local education authority continues to be the employer, governors will have 'hire and fire' and disciplinary powers over staff and will have individual liability for discriminatory or unfair practices which may well deter parents from serving. Parent governors may well find themselves to be the only members of the governing body who are not covered in such cases, the others being representatives of supporting bodies.

There has been a similar lack of enthusiasm to take part in the new accountability procedures through which parents can question the school's performance and possibly take corrective action. Parents continue to be interested in parent-teacher meetings and in written reports which *give an account* of what is going on in the school but public meetings at which headteachers are *held to account* for the school's performance have been poorly attended. For example, the Manor School, Cheadle, Cheshire, is exemplary in its determination to inform and involve parents and to enlist their support in ensuring that the children are given the education they deserve. It is worth quoting the school's experience of annual parents' meetings:

> The first Annual Parents Meeting was held before the end of the summer term to comply with the law. The second was held to ensure that the parents were able to consider the examination results at the earliest possible time, and more particularly because the Annual General Meeting of the Parent Teacher Association had to be held, according to the constitution, before the end of October. It was felt that it would be helpful to combine the two meetings since all parents and teachers are members of the Parent Teacher Association and governors are invited to their Annual General Meeting as a courtesy. In addition the Parent Teacher Association provides at least one glass of wine to persuade new parents to attend. Unfortunately the attendances were equally unsatisfactory on both occasions. At the first meeting there were 26 parents, the Head Boy, two teacher-governors, two parent-governors, four other governors and the Head Teacher.
>
> (Tomlinson 1988:16)

The Manor School's experience is simply an illustration of the findings of a number of studies which show the poor response from parents to the government invitation in the 1986 Act to call schools to account for what they do. Mahoney (1987) investigated experiences in Leicestershire and Derbyshire and found that in one-third of the annual meetings to receive school reports, fewer than 5 per cent of the parents on the school register attended. The attendance figure of around 5 per cent is confirmed in other studies.

In most schools the opportunities which have been increasingly provided for class teachers and parents to discuss the work of the individual child continue to command high support. Evidence is not yet available but it is reasonable to conjecture that the new complaints procedure for parents dissatisfied with the school's curriculum and assessment will be used to pursue individual discontent rather than the balance and relevance of the curriculum of the school as a whole.

Financial delegation

In several of its proposals the 1988 Act seeks to accelerate trends already evident in the education system, which can be traced back to the scheme in Hertfordshire when Newsom was Chief Education Officer. Over the past few decades there have been various trial schemes seeking to give schools greater autonomy in administering their own finances. Early experimental projects, of which the Inner London Education Authority's Alternative Use of Resources scheme is well documented, gave schools control over a sizeable portion of the budget. Leicestershire Community Schools (Phase III) had block budgeting from 1978. In 1982 Cambridgeshire initiated a trial scheme for local financial management of schools which is now regarded as a prototype in that schools were provided with a lump-sum allocation and were encouraged to become 'self-managing institutions'. A similar scheme, known as the school financial autonomy scheme, has developed in the metropolitan borough of Solihull since 1981.

Under the provisions of the 1988 Act all secondary schools and those primary schools with 200 pupils or more will have control over their budgets. In some areas, primary schools with fewer than 200 pupils will be included. There is, increasingly, an acceptance that control over the uses to which the school's finances are put will enable those making decisions on the development, organization, and operation of the school to have greater flexibility. It is also likely that the introduction of school-based budgeting will lead to greater awareness among teachers of the financial implications of educational decisions. Nevertheless, there is considerable concern among heads over how the complex operations of financial management are to be carried out. These misgivings arise largely from the fact that changes have been introduced without a planned programme to develop the capacities needed. Although the legislation provides that the governing body is charged with the responsibility for the school's budgets it is likely that in many cases the tasks involved will be delegated to the headteacher.

In the short term LEAs may be willing to offer assistance with staff development in this area but such provision is likely to be transitory and to focus on general principles rather than detailed procedures. Undoubtedly some schools will seek expert help from accountants or other financial consultants. In the past, however, schools have been accustomed to receiving in-service training and advisory support free of charge and may find the cost of outside professional services something of a shock. The expense for individual schools seeking to purchase financial and budgetary expertise from freelance consultants or from commercial enterprises may be more than they are willing to pay. Ways have to be found to provide for immediate assistance in actual budget preparation and, in the longer term, to help them to become self-sufficient in managing their own financial affairs. In the Education Management Unit of the University of Ulster the idea is being explored of using financial expertise in the Faculty of Business and Management, in conjunction with the Faculty of Education, to build training programmes and workshops for groups of schools around an actual budget prepared for a school typical of the group. Training which involves actual budget preparation should prove to be more economical than the engagement by individual schools of experts simply to do the budget for them.

An alternative approach, common in the independent sector, of appointing a bursar to manage the school's finances has already been adopted in several state schools. The delegation of financial management to schools will undoubtedly accelerate this trend, perhaps with the appointment of a bursar to a group of schools. One problem is that, traditionally, ancillary staff have been highly valued but seriously underpaid. School governors may be well advised to give serious consideration to recruiting and suitably remunerating someone with appropriate financial and possibly entrepreneurial competences, since the effective planning and utilization of the school's budget is one of their significant new accountabilities.

School governors

Headteachers and governors will be required to work closely together to ensure that the children are receiving the best possible education through optimum uses of resources. Their general responsibilities will include:

- the establishment of the educational needs and priorities of the school;
- a cost-benefit analysis of alternative allocation of funds to meet those priorities;
- the detailed deployment of resources;
- the monitoring of the impact of decisions taken;
- an evaluation of the effectiveness of programmes undertaken.

There is reason to hope that one of the beneficial outcomes of the Education Reform Act will be to give a stimulus to the development of close and rewarding partnership between the staff of schools and their governors. Many promising initiatives were already under way even before the Act. Following the publication of the White Paper, 'Better schools' (1985), the Society of Education Officers and the National Association of Head Teachers worked together to produce 'A training package: assisting governor education' (1986), recognizing that the role of a school governing body is to promote by its support, advice, oversight, and advocacy the well-being of the school, the progress of its pupils, and its integration with the community. The fulfilment of this task requires knowledge and understanding of the school and of the education system, together with skills in collaboration, communication and judgment.

The realization of the full potential of the partnership between schools and their governing bodies depends on two requirements being addressed:

- the proper preparation of governors to enable them to discharge their responsibilities effectively;
- acceptance by the school of its responsiblity to create circumstances in which the governing body will be encouraged to feel that it has a positive and constructive role to play.

The training of school governors is likely to be a growth industry as a consequence of The Education (No. 2) Act of 1986 closely followed by the 1988 Act and we can expect a spate of publications on the subject. The SEO/NAHT training package has been followed by 'The school governor's legal guide' produced by Lowe (1988), the Secretary of the Secondary Heads Association. The *Times Education Supplement* launched the first of eight instalments of its 'Governor's guide' in its issue of 14 October 1988 and has subsequently reissued all eight as a pack. Many LEAs have been quick to realize the need for providing help and general guidance to school governors. Not surprisingly, the emphasis in many of these is on functions, duties, and responsibilities and they deal mainly with factual information on such matters as the membership, procedures, and functions; procedures for appointment, promotion, and dismissal; the handling of redundancy; grievance and disciplinary procedures; and other matters relating to the legal context. These provide an essential knowledge base for the further development of governors in terms of the competences and attitudes required for schools and governors to work together harmoniously and productively.

The development in schools of positive attitudes towards school governors is therefore a key priority. The difficulty may lie in areas which traditionally have been regarded as the prerogative of the professional, for example, determining the curriculum and monitoring teaching standards. In the past, teachers have not seen themselves to be particularly accountable to governors in these matters. One of the conclusions Elliott (1981) reaches in a survey carried out as part of the Cambridge Accountability Project, is that the majority of teachers in the CAP schools felt neither individual nor collective accountability to governors. The fault may lie partially with the school. Kogan (1984) argues that the operation of the governing body is deeply influenced by the mode of operation of the school. Education has faced ill-informed criticism in the past few decades which perhaps could have been better countered by well-informed and involved governing bodies. Sallis (1988) makes the point that a failure to win the understanding of the ordinary well-intentioned majority would expose schools cruelly to those few who are interested in power. It can, indeed, be argued that a school gets the governors it deserves. Governors can be strong allies working with professionals for the good of the children. It is important that the governing body should be seen to be as much a part of the school community as the staff and the pupils.

The way forward

One undeniable consequence of the 1988 Act is that schools are facing unfamiliar problems and experiencing uncertainty over the future. The reality is that the educational system which is essentially complex, dynamic, and evolutionary is much more difficult to control by direct legislation than the government appears to believe. For example, the intention to shift the balance of power from teachers to parents by giving governing bodies more control over the curriculum is circumvented if, as has happened in some schools, a majority of parents elected as governors are in fact teachers. The concern of the government that teachers may have taken advantage of present legislation to gain a controlling interest or, at the least, a powerful influence on the way some schools are run is indicated by the setting up by the junior education minister of a national survey, to be conducted by the National Foundation for Educational Research, to discover the occupational backgrounds of Britain's 100,000 parent-governors. The evidence of history is that legislation can provide a facilitative framework, but that the framework must be capable of change as new understandings emerge. The ways in which the provisions of the 1944 Education Act came to be amended as the system evolved to meet the realities which existed gives hope that the new Act will achieve less than its supporters expect and cause less harm than many professionals fear. The 1944 Act provided for a tripartite system of education but that provision was short-lived because of the simple fact that babies refused to be born into the neat categories of academic, technical, and practical. More sadly, the high ambition of Butler to provide equal opportunity for all children failed to be realized because of the reality that educational opportunity depends more on social circumstance than on provision in schools.

Since many of the assumptions which implicitly underpin much of the Act rest on doubtful propositions, its provisions are flawed. A reason for optimism is that, as the system evolves over time, these flaws will become apparent and changes will be made. The legislation laid down in the Act does not, once and for all, determine an unchangeable future for an education system irretrievably moulded in the Baker pattern. As realities emerge, fresh rules and regulations can be introduced and appropriate practices adopted. Some five thousand amendments to the initial proposals were tabled and the Bill had a long and contentious passage in Parliament. Its passing in Parliament does not mark the end of the debate. The professional educator and concerned professional bodies will have important roles in determining the actual structures and procedures which are adopted. The Act may well be what professionals make of it. It is not a panacea for all ills as envisaged by some of its supporters nor is it a *coup de grace* for all that is good, as feared by some of its opponents. Sheila Doig, a serving headteacher, takes an optimistic view:

> It is so easy to become depressed and negative about the increasing burdens and restrictions placed upon us by Central Government but there are good things like Baker Days which must be seized upon as golden opportunities.
>
> (Doig 1988:6)

The positive view of the Education Reform Act is that it may well provide an impetus for accelerating existing development programmes and trends in education. It is idle to pretend that the education system has not had imperfections and that it has not been slow to change in order to meet changing social and economic circumstances. Many schools have been engaged in curriculum review and development but it has been deliberate policy to emphasize a school-based approach seeking the ideal of a self-evaluating, problem-solving organization identifying and adapting to specific needs. While retaining this ideal it may be that the time is ripe for a more co-ordinated and more outward-looking examination of the programmes offered within the system as a whole. Schools can well profit by taking greater account of, and attempting to reconcile, the various views of their clients, whether they be pupils, parents, industry, community, local and central government, or whoever. The notion of a national curriculum has definite merits provided its introduction does not stifle the creativity and responsiveness of the individual school seeking to meet its particular circumstances.

Similarly, most schools, though with varying success, have been purposefully developing stronger home–school links and encouraging greater involvement by parents. But it has to be admitted that these initiatives have largely been on the school's terms rather than those of the parents. There is nothing wrong with strengthening the parental hand. Equally, while there are real dangers in a belief that freedom of choice necessarily provides assurance of quality, there is, nevertheless, a strong argument for greater consumer awareness in education. Schools have become more aware of the need to sell education following a period of unprecedented debate and concern, and ebbing public confidence.

This is a lesson Baker might also have learned since he had overall responsibility for education. Too often he created an impression that the education system was a failed enterprise. It would be unusual to hear a chief executive of a large multiple constantly complaining about the poor quality of its product, the inefficiency of its staff, and the need to close some of its stores. It is interesting that, while the system as a whole is under criticism, most parents are satisfied with the individual school. In a Gallup Poll conducted for the *Daily Telegraph*, 1,028 parents of children at state school were interviewed during the period 28–30 September 1987. It was found that 84 per cent of parents were satisfied with their child's present school and that 93 per cent had had an acceptable choice of school. Nevertheless there is no cause for complacency. It is to be hoped that the Act will provide a challenge to schools which have been slow to develop the curriculum, to establish purposeful relationships with consumers or to project a positive image in the community. It will provide an opportunity and stimulus to those schools already involved. It can alert schools to the need to be even more outward-looking. At a time of greater accountability and more public scrutiny education may well require to demonstrate greater hard-headedness in the approach to change. Schools need to be seen to be more productive. Schools need to be seen to make better use of resources. Schools need to be seen to be more ready to adopt new technologies. Schools need to be seen to be more responsive to client needs. Schools need to be seen to be more competitive.

Implications for management

The Education Reform Act will have considerable impact on the way schools are managed. In particular, there is general agreement that it will have widespread implications for senior teachers. There is less agreement on what the true implications are and the nature of the response that is required. Addressing the Sixteenth Annual Conference of the British Educational Management and Administration Society, the General Secretary of the Secondary Heads Association depicted a possible model of the Baker headteacher based on the image of the headteacher of the independent school. The picture that emerged was that they would be public-relations figures much concerned with the image of the school; that they would work more closely with governors than with teachers; that they would be involved more with finance than with curriculum; be more directly concerned with pupil intake than with pupil progress; shrewd rather than scholarly, well groomed, personable, charismatic, and dynamic.

This picture is not inconsistent with the growing tendency to regard the headteacher as general manager or chief executive. It is easy to see how the new Act might reinforce such a concept of the headteacher. Undoubtedly new functions of a largely managerial nature will devolve from local authority level to school level. There is a real danger that the responsibility for carrying out the specific tasks involved will come to reside solely with the headteacher. Thus the headteacher would be required to become a financial manager, a public relations manager, a personnel manager, a sales manager, a legal expert, a labour-relations expert, an advertising expert, a media expert and so on. It is obvious nonsense. The headteacher already carries wide-ranging responsibilities and the role demands a daunting array of abilities. A recent appraisal of secondary schools by HMI (1988) concluded that the most effective schools are led by 'heads with considerable professional, personal, managerial, administrative and political skills'. Indeed! One is reminded of Goldsmith's village schoolmaster: '. . . and still the wonder grew/ That one small head could carry all he knew.'

Nevertheless, while it may be expecting altogether too much of the headteachers, the statement helps implicitly to identify some of the areas in which they require to be effective. The headteacher's role must not be reduced to purely administrative and managerial functions to the exclusion of the all-important task of providing professional academic leadership. It is certainly what teachers expect of the headteacher. An indication of this is the clear statement from the NAS/UWT that it is their view that the head's main task must be to provide professional leadership. It is significant that similar views have been expressed by concerned parent bodies.

Yet there is already a number of danger signs. It is a common complaint among headteachers that increasingly they spend more and more time behind their desks, less and less time in the classroom; more and more time in 'boundary management', less and less time in contact with their colleagues within the school. It is also ominous that already courses are being set up offering training for headteachers in narrow specialist skills and techniques. Clearly, as a number of new administrative functions have been devolved to school level, there must be a response by the schools, and this requires training of different kinds at different levels. Equally clearly, the headteachers will have to accept new accountabilities in areas which may be unfamiliar and perhaps alien to them. But it is the central premiss of this book that what the head-teacher needs is not training in specific techniques but a broad understanding of the concepts, language and principles required to monitor and control the activities necessary to carry out the new functions and to evaluate the outcomes.

It is the brief of the headteacher to hold ultimate accountability for all the work of the school which already includes a wide range of specialist activities. Such a person is unlikely to be a specialist in all subjects yet has to be able to encourage, guide and monitor the teaching in all areas of the curriculum. Headteachers need to be clear about the processes, purposes, and expected outcomes and to be able to speak the language equally of the mathematician and the historian. It is, similarly, not necessary for them to become experts in budgeting, in the law of labour relations, in marketing and so on. But they cannot remain ignorant of these fields. Nor is it enough simply to delegate responsibility and leave it there.

The argument here is that it is possible to identify four requirements:

• Schools require to meet the challenges of the new Act.
• There needs to be a whole school response which may require a change in the traditional culture in education.
• Heads need to acquire knowledge and understanding in new areas of accountability.
• Staff carrying out new specific responsibilities will require immediate and intensive training.

There is no doubt that the major task for headteachers is to ensure that the school as a whole realizes the challenges it faces, and that all staff work as a team to meet these challenges. The responsibility cannot be left to the headteacher and cannot be delegated to single individuals. It cannot be expected, for example, that the appointment of a member of staff as public-relations officer, as recommended by one team of management consultants, will be effective unless all members of staff accept their responsibility to be more market-oriented. It is not unknown for teachers to take an attitude: 'You are paid to do it, so you do it.' If such an appointment is made it must be recognized that the role is to co-ordinate the efforts of the school as a whole and to provide administrative support.

All staff must realize that the nature of the environment in which schools operate is more demanding and that much more critical judgements of performance, will be made. Schools have traditionally received weak feedback on performance characterized by innocuous inspection, absence of complaints procedures, supportive non-critical parent-teacher associations, funding unrelated to performance, and protected intakes. The Education Reform Act changes all this. It has been suggested earlier that schools need to become more hard-headed, more productive, more competitive, more responsive and so on. The theme of this book is that in order to effect the necessary changes, an understanding is essential of how the provisions in the new legislation will impact on the school and its organization, ethos, procedures, and ways of behaving. The role of the headteacher in relation to these changes is to provide the necessary leadership.

References

DES (1986) *Better Schools*, London: HMSO.

DES Inspectorate of Schools (1988) *Secondary Schools: an Appraisal Based on Inspections in England 1982–86*, London: HMSO.

Doig, S. (1988) 'A head's month: one head's look at management', *Management in Education*, vol. 2, no 1, Spring.

Elliott, J., Bridges, D., Ebbitt, D., Gibson, R., and Nias, J. (1981) School Accountability, London: Grant McIntyre.

Gallup (1988) *Omnibus study on education*, Table 13.9.

Hansard (1987) *Official Reports*, Sixth Series Parliamentary Debates, vol. 123, 23 November–4 December.

Kogan, M. (ed.) (1984) *School Governing Bodies*, London: Heinemann.

Lowe, C. (1988) *The School Governor's Legal Guide*, New Malden: Croner Publications.

Mahoney, T. (1988) *Governors and Parents*, Nottingham: Workers Educational Association.

NAHT (1986) *A Training Package: Assisting Governor Education*, Haywards Heath: NAHT Publications.

Pring, R. (1988), 'Privatisation', *Educational Management and Administration*, vol. 16, no 2, Summer.

Sallis, J. (1988) *Schools, Parents, and Governors: A New Approach to Accountability*, London: Routledge.

Tomlinson, H. (1988) 'Management in Action 2: Annual Parents' Meetings', *Management in Education*, vol. 2, no. 1, Spring.

Chapter two

Resource management in schools: some conceptual and practical considerations

Michael Strain

At the heart of the task of management is the obligation to get things done. Not any thing at any price, but the right things done well and thriftily. Resources are the means whereby this central management function is carried out, the means whereby we get things done. The whole burden of recent professional and political preoccupations in respect of the management of education has been concerned with questions of resource management. Are we doing the right things in the curriculum of schools, in the range of course provision in the post-school sector: Core Curriculum, NCVQ? Are we doing them well, or well enough: GCSE, appraisal, assessment? Are we doing them wastefully: Audit Commission? This chapter seeks to illuminate discussion of questions of this kind by exploring some fundamental aspects of resource management in education in ways which are both analytical and practical. It is, therefore, concerned both with how things are and with what we can do about them.

Concepts and values

More than mere academic self-indulgence requires that some consideration should first be given to the concept of resources itself. This is because the form in which we see and construct an understanding of a situation will limit and often determine the response we make in terms of subsequent action. Concepts shape actions. Second, and consequently, if we are seriously concerned to take effective practical action in a matter we should be prepared to re-examine the concepts we use. And yet we cannot simply jettison and replace concepts like so many pre-cooked dishes in a supermarket; concepts, to be usable in action, must be fitted for and, in some necessary sense, derived from elements of the situation in which action is contemplated. Concepts shape actions; but actions are meaningful by virtue of particular personal situations. Therefore concepts must be grounded in the salient and significant elements of the situation in which action is located. The

15

practical implication of this argument is that the concepts we choose to employ should be related to the role of the actor in a particular situation. Useful concepts provide a logical link between the questions 'Where am I?' (the situation) and 'What am I doing here?' (the actor's role).

If the conceptual linkage is adequate it will provide a basis upon which to answer the urgent practical question 'What am I to do here and now?' An engineer, a transportation planner, and a motorist are each actors at different points of time in relation to a particular stretch of road. They have to do with the same reality. Yet they employ vastly different conceptualizations of the road. The engineer uses a three-dimensional model since his role requires him to attend not only to the surface but to the substructure. His task is to ensure that a sprawling three-dimensional structure, formed of a variety of mineral and chemical aggregates, holds together, having regard to the known or predictable qualities of climate, geology, and usage. By contrast the transportation planner and the motorist are interested only in the surface; their concept of the road is thus two-dimensional. Whereas the engineer employs an essentially static model, the planner requires a dynamic model replicating surface traffic movements at different times of a typical day. The motorist uses an even simpler model or perceptual image of the ribbon of carriageway along which he drives. Each adopts a very different concept of the road; in each case the concept is framed by the role assumed by three different actors in respect of the same stretch of road.

The argument can be taken a step further if we turn now to the more specific issue of resource management in education. The government apparently believes that the education service can and should be managed according to the same criteria of efficiency, effectiveness and productivity as any other economic undertaking. In accordance with its broad social and economic philosophy, education should be regarded as a publicly financed commodity. Commodity replaces service as a core concept, so that the so-called disciplines of free market exchange may be introduced, to regulate the supply and demand of the product, in place of the former mechanisms of bureaucratic planning and regulatory control. As with a commercial company producing and selling tangible products in the high street, central control is retained for the key functions of product specification, quality control, and corporate resource allocation. Within this framework, each outlet, by presenting itself as a marketplace for the sale of commodities, becomes the mechanism for determining levels of supply and demand via prices. Consumers, by exercising choice, can freely signal their satisfaction or dissatisfaction with what is for sale. They can say whether it is overpriced much more clearly and effectively than by the cumbersome apparatus of the electoral process, local government planning, and statutory consultations. Education as commodity is embedded in the

1988 Education Act (MacLure 1988). The adoption of this concept leads to the formulation of an organizational structure of distributed powers and responsibilities quite different from the existing framework which was developed in response to the 1944 Act (Brighouse 1988). In the 1944 Act the key concept of public education as a service required central government to ensure that an appropriate service was delivered. The particular form and practical execution of that service was the responsibility of local authorities representing teachers, parents and beneficiaries. Central Government now seeks radically to alter and redistribute responsibility among the traditional partners (Ranson 1988) because it wishes to give practical effect to its belief that education will become more relevant and more efficiently delivered if it is used by participants as a commodity to be bought and sold rather than as a service paternalistically provided. An underlying concept or model of reality has been replaced so that ensuing action may take place in a changed form to meet new purposes. It is this that makes the ERA a *Reform* Act, not the specific stipulations regarding curriculum, management, and organization, which are only limited and partial expressions of a new conceptual framework. Nevertheless, implementation of these proposed new arrangements presents challenges of a distinctively new kind to many in the education service. A range of practical aspects and implications of these various challenges are addressed by contributors to this volume. Here an attempt is made to examine how the way in which we conceptualize the task of resource management can limit or expand the field of available purposeful actions.

Resources are usually thought of as a set of materials available for purposeful use. The notion is easily capable of extension so that the set of materials may include, as well as inanimate objects, human beings whose time and personal attributes may be put to particular uses at a specifiable cost. The task of resource management is concerned accordingly with the techniques and processes necessary to ensure the effective deployment of finite available resources. The notion is commonplace and is regularly reinforced by the terms and assumptions underlying everyday political and economic discussion. It is essentially a concept of objectification: people and things are taken to be objects usable in a determinate process with specifiable outcomes. Operations where inputs and their necessary mix are known and linked definably to particular outcomes lend themselves most readily to this conceptualization of the resource task. Thus industrial and commercial operations, where outcomes are identified as completed transactions in a market, namely the sale of a product, are managed successfully in terms of efficient resource allocation by the application of analytical decision techniques derived from an objectifying concept of resources.

Cost–benefit analysis, output budgeting, a variety of investment appraisal and costing approaches are examples of such methods, widely practised in industrial, commercial, and many public-sector enterprises. The shortcomings of these methods are well known to economists who have over the past century developed the theoretical foundations and conceptual models from which these practical analytical techniques derive. Their inadequacy for many fields of social action lies in their essential objectivity. Objectification makes possible prediction, calculation and control. Yet metaphors which objectify reality in this way also require that what is being examined should exhibit a number of peculiarly 'unreal' features.

We have to assume that the social world or the institutional component which we seek to manage is essentially a static, intrinsically unchanging entity, subject only to fixed laws governing its organic development, and change effects attributable to factors outside the institution itself. The institution is imagined as existing in a stationary state in which change occurs as a result of changes in its internal composition or changes in external conditions. The assumption is convenient in that it makes possible prediction of the consequences of deliberate changes either to the form of the institution, for example, new managerial structures, or to the external conditions in which it operates, for example, open enrolment of pupils. But it is quite unrealistic in that it excludes the possibility of some new element being introduced by the imagination and conscious choice of individuals inside or outside the institution. Teachers might behave differently and unpredictably in their more directively managed professional situation, and parents too might respond unexpectedly to their newly conferred freedom to choose a school for their children. Realism in the chosen metaphor is attenuated so that prediction and control of ensuing events become more manageable. Supplementing this pale and diluted metaphor of lived social experience is the closely related assumption that social change can be regarded as a moving succession of fixed stationary states along a time continuum which we call the calendar. Time is conceived as linear space so that the moving kaleidoscope of human actions can be reduced for purposes of control and measurement to measurable entities – utilization of time, space and material resources. With this conceptual device the effort and physical resources employed when two men labour in an acre of land for ten hours to produce a hundredweight of tomatoes can be taken as equal to the disposition of resources involved when four men labour in a field of the same size for half the time with an equivalent product. If the output of one arrangement is greater than that of the other then the arrangement is seen to be more productive. If the same product can be achieved by reducing the quantity of inputs in one of these arrangements, then an increase in efficiency can be said to have been achieved. It matters nothing whether the two sets of men are working in adjacent fields, in the same economic and cultural context, or not. By making time and space coordinates, human events can be both sequential and coexistent. By divorcing events from the historical flux in which meanings are constructed by those labouring in fields or teaching in schools, the objective value of those actions can be calculated and compared by the application of a universal calculus. Action, in this conceptualization, is made timeless, stationary, and therefore ahistorical, so that its value can be measured. The measurable supplants the meaningful as the basis of valuation.

The third feature of this objectifying conceptualization of social action is the requirement of one-way causation. The inputs quantifiable on the time/space axes are regarded as not only efficient cause of the produced outputs, but are themselves insulated from any reflexive effects of products. This entails an assumption that the subjective experience of actors in any production process can never be taken into account as a casual factor in subsequent production. In our two imaginary fields of tomato growing, the satisfaction experienced by one group and not enjoyed, for whatever reasons, by the other is excluded as a possible or putative input in a subsequent day's labour. In real life, it is widely recognized that experiential factors crucially affect output; in the practice of industrial relations and in social psychology much effort is devoted to resolving questions arising from this general observation. Social action is inherently reflexive. Inputs, human and material, are continuously being changed by the reflexive process of social interactions; individuals acquire skills as a result of their experience as actors; objects, tools, machines, become worn, repaired, modified, and developed as a direct consequence of man's involvement with them as necessary adjuncts of their conscious activity in pursuit of particular goals. Moreover, there is a generally available, relatively non-technical language and analytical form in which we describe and explain these phenomena, namely, historical narrative. In their attempts to understand and direct the future course of their personal and institutional lives, men confront their time-bounded mortality and their limited capacity to exploit the material world. This dynamic, time-bounded, reflexive dimension is omitted from heuristic and explanatory models based upon objectifications of social reality. This omission should give cause for concern when such a model is built into detailed legislation regarding education. The Act, by its philosophy and by its detailed provision, aims to increase efficiency, raise standards, and enlarge the scope and power of parental choice. As we have seen, these objectives are, in the government's view, causally interrelated. The mechanism of market freedom is expected naturally to promote efficiency and productivity. This fundamental assumption, deriving as we have seen from a particular concept of social processes, underpins its choice of appropriate new procedures. Accordingly the Act seeks to redistribute management responsibilities and develop new mechanisms of control and direction. Yet these beliefs, though widely influential and efficacious in other fields, are now assumed to be equally valid in the field of education where, more than in almost any other, little is known about the relationship between inputs and outputs. Precise specification of desired outcomes is, if not unattainable, far from being attained, and benefits attributable to the education system are diverse, and frequently conjoint (Thomas and Simkins 1987). It is therefore impossible in practice to know in advance which benefits will be lost if particular components of the process are eliminated or under-resourced.

We should not, therefore, in our response to the 1988 Education Act, accept the conceptualization of the education process implicit there, along with the stipulated procedures which heads, teachers and others are obliged to carry out as part of their professional duties. We may not wish to subvert the Act; indeed, there are already indications that some aspects of the legislation will strengthen the education system in relation to other claimants upon public funds and will enhance the capacity of schools to serve the children and young people to whom teachers owe and acknowledge a professional commitment. The next section will explore how far a different concept of resources from the static, objectifying assumptions underlying the Act's philosophy is possible, and how alternative conceptualisations of the resource management task can facilitate a more humane and educationally effective approach to management in response to the Act's stipulations. The attempt is, in short, to make the Act work constructively for the education service.

The new mechanisms of local management

The new arrangements for the management of schools introduced by the 1988 Act are conveniently considered under the following headings:

- Formula funding
- Open enrolment
- Performance indicators
- Financial delegation
- Staffing

The purpose of the discussion which follows will be not only to exemplify some of the general and theoretical observations developed earlier, but also to present some practical proposals for implementing the Act's new arrangements in ways which preserve enduring educational values.

Formula funding

In future, the formula determining the distribution of resources to schools within any LEA will be uniform. Moreover, across all LEAs, the criteria upon which such formulae may be established will be generally applicable to all. This should produce greater national uniformity among the patterns of expenditure adopted by LEAs, though the levels of expenditure on education will continue to be strongly influenced by historical and political factors as well as by national policies for local government expenditure and methods of grant distribution (Gibson and Watt 1987). The government's insistence that formulae must be based on 75 per cent of available funds being distributed on a *per capita* principle will itself ensure greater uniformity, once the effect of year-on-year adjustments to remove historic differences has worked itself through. But the chief interest in this new arrangement is the limited 25 per cent scope offered to local authorities to weight the distribution of school funds to provide for particular needs which may vary from school to school (DES 1988: 22–5). These may include compensation for diseconomies of scale, (as in the case of the small primary school), provision for SEN pupils, positive discrimination to develop multicultural and compensatory education, or the steering of funds to promote adult and continuing education in areas of social disadvantage or high endemic unemployment. If schools are to maximize the inflow of LEA-provided funds, they will need to develop in their staff a sensitivity to, and increased awareness of, local policy regarding educational priorities. This need not imply a merely passive stance for the school within the new division of labour, for, as the LEA assumes a strategic, resourcing, and monitoring role, with management and responsibility for delivery devolved to schools and their governing bodies, so policy-making should now assume a much more reciprocal and reflexive character, with proactive and successful schools contributing significantly to the identification of needs and providing an experiential basis for the construction of local policies. Thus responsive and successful schools will signpost the desirable direction of policy and steer perceptive and electorally sensitive policy-makers by the same process that they stake their claim to available local resources.

Open enrolment

In future, existing rationing devices to control pupil admissions, except those based on selection by ability, will be replaced by the concept of the standard number. This represents the maximum number of pupils in a year group which a school may be required to admit. It is designed to enable parents to choose more freely amongst schools in a particular neighbourhood. Its effectiveness will depend upon the availability of more than one suitable school within convenient travelling distance; and, since no change has been made regarding existing provision of free school transport, the operation of the free market principle will continue to be curtailed by the effect of limited subsidies. It is a strategy which can only succeed in fairly densely populated conurbations. Even so, there will be a significant proportion of families for whom the marginal cost of transport will be prohibitive and who will, therefore, be effectively excluded from these new opportunities for exercising choice. In Northern Ireland, where the majority of schools serve sparsely populated communities, and where the 'education market' is fragmented by religious denominations, sex, and academic selection processes, open enrolment is most obviously a device to accelerate the rationalization of underused school premises (DENI 1988: 11–12). None the less, pupil admissions must now figure more prominently in a school's management agenda. Schools will need to consider whether to collaborate with other schools and to identify the community they can jointly and realistically hope to serve or to compete with others for the market sector whose custom is to be sought.

Just as formula funding requires a school to become more involved in the external policy-making environment, so open enrolment should prompt schools to specify for themselves how pupils' educational needs will be provided for and how the message regarding what is on offer can more sharply and persuasively be conveyed to their local public. It is important for managers in schools to recognize that neither of these measures imprisons them in circumstances and an ineluctable vice of external control. There is scope for initiative, for negotiation with LEAs and for active involvement in awareness raising, both within the school and the neighbouring community. This relationship itself is something to be explored creatively and developed practically. Public relations need not be manipulative or narrowly framed on commercial lines, but can be a means of developing parent–school involvement, informing parents of available choices, of their potential role in their children's education, and of creating for the school a vital and mutually enriching function in the life of a wider community.

Performance indicators

Of the five elements in the Act's local management package this is the most difficult to offer comment upon at this stage. Performance indicators are signals intended to give an indication as to whether a school is performing as it should. There are two kinds of problem associated with this approach to generating management information:

- For whom are the signals meant?
- What aspect of performance are the signals about?

If we make a list of interested groups likely to be concerned with a school's performance, we will find that their interest produces a different focus of concern. Consider, for example, the following groups and their likely interests.

The local general public will be interested in:

- the behaviour of pupils outside the school premises, for example in local shops;
- the level and type of community related activity in the curriculum;
- the relevance and success of the school's curriculum in providing for the local labour market;
- the incidence of vandalism in the vicinity and in general;
- the school's costs in comparison with those of other schools.

Parents will be interested in all those issues, plus:

- levels of examination success;
- the range and type of subjects available;
- school discipline;
- the range of extra-curricular activities;
- the quality of personal relations between staff and pupils;
- class size;
- quality and availability of material resources.

Governing body/LEA will be interested in all those issues above, plus:

- the efficiency with which resources are being utilized;
- the extent to which the aims and objectives set out in the school's policy document are being achieved;
- the extent to which all pupils are fulfilling their educational potential;
- the extent to which all pupils are being equally provided for;
- the school's all-round achievement in relation to other schools locally and nationally;
- the extent to which the school's performance matches the LEA's educational strategy.

A school's teaching staff will be interested, in varying degrees, in all these aspects of the school's performance, but only a few of them will be of any direct relevance to their specific teaching functions in relation to particular pupils in particular areas of curriculum. For these they will be looking to the recommendations of the Task Group on Assessment and Testing. They will be concerned to know whether any of the data to be collected on pupil performance will have some diagnostic value, capable of helping them direct their skills more closely to meet the needs of individual pupils. If only raw data on pupil and school performance is to be collected, and if this is to be the basis of external assessment of their own competence and of their school's efficiency and effectiveness, they will legitimately question whether such a signalling system can say anything worth knowing about what schools actually do for their pupils. Information on costs is readily quantifiable and should be intelligibly made public. But such information describes only the volume and type of inputs expended and can, at best, be only a crude index of thrift or wastefulness. Information on pupil attainment, unless adjusted to take account of the multiplicity of factors which affect pupil learning, will convey more about the quality of pupils enrolling than about what happened to them whilst attending a particular school.

In the short to medium term, this provision of the Act should perhaps encourage schools to address and respond more openly than they have felt it necessary to do in the past to the questions likely to be of interest to the three groups identified above. Their concerns will be more meaningfully and more satisfactorily met by an approach to accountability which seeks to inform, explain and illuminate, for the benefit of those groups, the unique value of a particular school in the lives of its pupils and the community thus served. An attempt by teachers more fully and more intelligibly to explain the work they do, and the benefits sought and achieved by their pupils, will contribute developmentally to the quality and effectiveness of their educative task. Summary statistics and the tabulating of raw data will do little to answer most of the questions requiring attention. Once again, it is worth emphasizing that the Act does not limit accountability to the publication of crude measures of performance. The obligation imposed by the Act can be a starting point for a much richer and genuinely informative process of reporting and the establishment of mutual dialogue between schools and those they serve.

Financial delegation

This is perhaps the most far-reaching of all the Act's provisions. Although ostensibly it deals with the delegation of financial authority from the LEA to the school, its implications for the way in which schools will be most effectively managed are much more extensive and potentially radical. Each LEA must submit a scheme of financial delegation for approval by the Secretary of State. As with the arrangements for formula funding, the government criteria, to which all LEA schemes must conform, are set out in Circular 7/88 (DES 1988: 11–20). The government's clear intention is that there should be as much delegation to the school level as is feasible, although in all schemes a number of categories of expenditure, such as capital building, school meals subsidies, and school transport, will remain in the control of the LEA. The practical effect of delegated powers is that virement can be exercised between one category of expenditure and another. Estimates of anticipated expenditure on one item, say teaching staff, may be altered once the school's annual budget has been allocated, so that, in the event, less may be spent on teachers and more on equipment than was assumed in the LEA formula or anticipated by the school itself when estimates were being prepared. In other words, schools themselves can make real choices as to how available resources are to be deployed in pursuit of chosen educational objectives. Of course, there will be limitations upon the school's capacity to exercise choice. It is the very essence of choice that it is both effective and limited in its operation. For choice to be effective means that to choose A rather than B makes a difference to the subsequent course of events. But if the exercise of choice were not inherently limited by force of circumstances and the constraint of what at any moment for any actor is possible, if all imaginable courses of action were capable of being enacted, then all could be put into effect and no choice would be necessary. Choice takes place in imagination, upon a ground of uncertainty, between opposing vistas of possibility and constraining necessity.

In practical terms, the limitations upon a school's freedom to choose manifest themselves in two ways. There will be explicit and readily defined limitations in the form of legal and quasi-legal impositions. In addition to the expenditure items excluded from the delegated budget, schools will be bound by legislation on employment practices, health and safety, sex and race discrimination, and the regulations governing financial administration by charitable and public bodies. A second, much less easily defined class of limitations derives from the economic and social dimensions of choice within organizations. By this is meant those inherent and problematic features of choice which are of especial interest to economists and sociologists and of particular relevance to the study of management. These include, for example, information, structure, politicization, and staffing.

Information

The information necessary for making prudent and advantageous choices is often inadequate and always costly to gather and to make accessible to decision-makers. Out of any particular array of possible choices, the limitation of costly, desirable information will make some choices seem more risky or less attractive than might have been the case if more information had been more cheaply or freely available. This dimension of choice, frequently overlooked in practice, should encourage organizations to look carefully at their information requirements – the desirable form and extent of their management information system (MIS). Performance indicators will form part of a system, as will data on staff, enabling curriculum change to steer the use of available resources for staff development. Pupils, too, will form an essential subheading, facilitating a diagnostic approach to teaching strategies. Policy review will be accomplished more satisfactorily and with lower costs in staff time if the available MIS has been designed to serve the monitoring and review activities of the school, thus allowing the school more readily and more constructively to answer increasing demands to account for the school's performance.

Structure

Extending the range and scope of choices to be made by an organization will usually enlarge the number of people involved in the decision process. Sometimes more will actively participate in decision-taking; frequently more people will contribute administratively or in an advisory capacity. Consequently, more elaborate structures and more formalized procedures will need to be developed to sustain and carry through decisions and their implementation. More meetings, more records and an expanded data-base will be required. But a more positive emphasis is possible. If financial delegation is going to assist the school to become more efficient, effective, and responsive to clients, and if, in the words of the Secretary of State, 'schools and colleges will be free to make their own decisions on spending priorities and to develop in their own way' (Haviland 1988: 2), then delegation cannot stop at the level of the headteacher and governing bodies. The necessary corollary of delegation is participation. The necessary delegation of specific powers from the headteacher to school committees, departments, and individual members of staff and the active participation of all staff in decision-making processes should be pervasive characteristics of school management post-1988. In this way the teaching role itself will be enhanced to a powerful and enriching degree. Just as pupils, if the objectives of GCSE are achieved, will no longer be passive recipients of learning but active learners, with increased responsibility for their own learning under the supervision and direction of teachers, so teachers themselves can become active participants in the management processes of the school. The new roles and relationships that will be created among teachers and between teachers and the senior staff in schools, could lead to a much more radical reform of schools as institutions than explicitly provided for in the Act itself.

Politicization

Greater autonomy in financial matters has brought with it a requirement for greater accountability. This contextual necessity to respond more fully to the expressed needs of the community, to account for the efficiency and effectiveness with which schools spend money and implement nationally determined curricula, and to report formally to governing bodies on their activities, will be a powerful, if often latent, influence limiting the range and character of choices available. In effect, teachers will be increasingly constrained in their consideration of available choices by their perception of what is acceptable to the local community and to their political representatives. This, as we have seen earlier, is not in itself undesirable or necessarily dysfunctional. Indeed, it is probable that the objectives of a contemporary, secular, client-focused curriculum cannot be achieved without the introduction of such a constraint upon the traditional professional autonomy of the teacher. The technical and vocational outcomes to which the whole education system, from primary school to university, is being directed are clear manifestations of the necessity for such a shift. But it is important to recognize the broader context and explanatory field of these changes, for they represent a decisive move to accelerate the politicization of the education system. The traditional autonomy of the teacher, the model of the education process and its individualistic humane purpose, was a product and legacy of the churches and religious groups who defined and controlled the functions of educational establishments from the seventh until the late nineteenth century. The distinctive technology of the school, a pupil with a teacher in a room, equipped with writing materials, has remained unchanged in Western Europe since around 650 BC. The progressive introduction since 1944 of electronic aids, for example, the tape recorder, the TV, the VCR, and the computer, and the articulation of wider educational aims have heralded the need to develop a new pedagogy, a new curriculum and a new relationship between educational institutions and society. The then Secretary of State, Kenneth Baker, recognized that a combination of 'managerialism' and consumerism grafted upon the culture of schooling could forcefully promote these developments (Haviland 1988:2). Standards, it is hoped, will be raised by the Act's purpose which is 'to secure delegation and to widen choice'. There is an indication here that the newly manager-ialized, professional role of the teacher is designed to enable the school to respond more directly to the demands of a newly empowered consumer/parent. Teacher autonomy is henceforth a functional, not a ritualistic conferment. A similar transformation is visible in the new school/LEA relationship. By its subordination in the 1944 arrangement to a paternalistic, providing LEA, both the school and the teacher were insulated from direct political and parental involvement. The 1988 provisions remove much of this insulation and the school is exposed much more openly to the pressures of community and individual demand.

Staffing

Here, finally, we come up against the central paradox of financial delegation. On the one hand, the school is to have extensive powers to exercise choice in the deployment of resources, yet the school's major resource, its teaching staff, is being subjected to much more stringent conditions governing their employment, their use of time in professional activity, and their conduct of teaching within a centrally defined curriculum. What sense are we to make of this paradox and what scope remains for managers in schools to sustain the professionalism of their staff, whilst at the same time achieving efficiency and effectiveness according to criteria which will be increasingly determined by central authorities?

In fact, four key parameters of the education process are now to be determined by agencies outside the school, with minimal teacher representation.

Governing body	Appointment and dismissal of teachers	How many teachers in a school
DES/NCC	National curriculum	What is to be taught
DES/CLEA	Conditions of service	How teacher time is spent
DES/LEA	Appraisal of teachers; Assessment of pupils	How teaching and learning is to be valued

Governing bodies are explicitly required to exercise their delegated powers 'in a manner which is consistent with the implementation of the national curriculum, with the statutory requirements relating to the curriculum as a whole . . . and . . . with the LEA's curriculum policy' (DES 1988: 35). In addition to their other statutory responsibilities for employees, they are subject to the Teachers' Pay and Conditions Act 1987 and to the requirements of a national scheme of monitoring and evaluation (DES 1988: 31, 45). All the major instruments of control of the education production process are mapped here and they are located outside the school. In a manufacturing analogy, we might say that the volume, type and quality of resources, their deployment and use, product specification, and quality control are all here determined by central and local government. Only marketing and a certain amount of discretion in the deployment of resources at the plant level are left to teachers and governing bodies. It is here then, in these discretionary margins, that the potential contribution of teachers must be identified, developed and effectively applied.

As we have already seen, the legislation assumes that the imposition of a production/commodity model of the education system and a detailed specification of the parameters of its operation can by themselves change the character of education to be provided and ensure greater economy and effectiveness. But knowledge and understanding of the discrete components of the process, the production function, are largely the preserve of teachers themselves. Knowledge of the necessary conditions of pupil learning, of the requisite material resources and how they can be utilized; skill to control and influence the quality of classroom interactions, to establish an enabling relationship based on trust, mutual respect and self-discipline; judgement in the allocation and prioritization of available time for particular learning projects: all these remain in the hands of teachers themselves. Many of these essential components of the process are formatively shaped by decisions regarding the use of time, decisions which are organizationally and most explicitly given expression in the school timetable. This suggests that the following areas for research and development might extend and refine professional knowledge of the production process, which, unlike a physical production process, cannot be removed from the control of the teachers and learners who jointly engage in it:

Timetabling: the principles of good timetable composition could be explored through comparative studies. How far does the pattern of resource allocation embodied there match the aims and priorities enshrined in school and LEA policy?
Use of teacher time: intra-institutional and intra-classroom studies of time utilization would attempt to answer questions such as: How is non-teaching teacher time spent? How is teacher time within the classroom distributed? How far are habitual patterns compatible with curricular objectives and the espoused school policy?
The resource mix: what balance of human and material resources will optimize the deployment of available cash resources in pursuit of discrete learning objectives within a chosen complement of curricular aims? Only by a more thorough exploration of the 'technology' of organized learning can the relative marginal values of alternative resource dispositions be accurately identified. And it is these marginal values that should guide institutional decision-making when virement between staff, books, visits, equipment, and so on is being considered.

In attempting to answer questions of this kind and by implementing the appropriate managerial response, the authority of the professional practitioner and education manager is practically unchallengeable. Yet in the new post-1988 politicized system of education, authority no longer derives from conferment of status but must be earned by the possession and demonstration of technical expertise. The maintenance of humane values which have characterized European education since classical times depends upon teachers appropriating these necessary skills. In this way education can continue to be practised as a service given to persons who are socially and historically interdependent rather than produced as a commodity to be offered for sale in a market place of independently competing consumers.

References

Brighouse, T. (1988) 'Politicizing the manager or managing the politicians? – Can the headteacher succeed where the education officer failed?', *Education Management and Administration*, vol. 16, no. 2, Summer.

DES (1988) Circular 7/88, Education Reform Act: Local Management of Schools, London: HMSO.

Department of Education Northern Ireland (DENI) (1988) *Education Reform in Northern Ireland: The Way Forward*, Belfast: HMSO.

Gibson J. and Watt P. (1987) 'A model of education expenditure and change in English local authorities', in H. Thomas and T. Simkins (eds) *Economics and the Management of Education: Emerging Themes*, Lewes: Falmer Press.

Haviland J. (1988) *Take Care, Mr Baker*, London: Fourth Estate

MacLure S (1988) *Education Re-formed*, London: Hodder & Stoughton.

Ranson, S. (1988) 'From 1944 to 1988: education, citizenship, democracy', *Local Government Studies*, vol. 4, no.1. February.

Thomas, H. and Simkins T. (1987) *Economics and the Management of Education: Emerging Themes*, Lewes: Falmer Press.

Chapter three

Local financial management

Denise McAlister and Michael Connolly

The Education Reform Act (1988) proposes, among a number of other fundamental reforms, that there should be greater delegation to schools of responsibility for financial and other aspects of management. This has become popularly known, and increasingly referred to, as Local Management in Schools (LMS). The Act proposes that each local authority should devise a formula for allocating funds to each of its schools and that financial delegation shall be applied to the allocated funds of all secondary schools and to primary schools above 200 pupils. As indicated in the appendix these changes must be implemented by 1994 at the latest, and might well be operational before that date. Clearly the changes contained in the Act will have important implications for school managers.

The purpose of this chapter is to explore some of these anticipated developments. Initially it outlines some of the key features of the system of delegated management as currently articulated by the government. It then focuses on the mechanisms by which LEAs will arrive at the budget allocation for each school, and concludes by considering its operational and behavioural consequences for school managers. Two related aspects are examined, namely, how to undertake a budgetary exercise and how this process may be used in order to enhance the management function generally.

Financial management initiative

Decentralized financial management has been a feature of the Thatcher government's approach to reform of public sector management generally. The current wave of interest in financial management practices within central government arises from the financial management initiative (FMI). Launched in May 1982, the initiative emphasized three key areas of public sector management: management by objectives, accountable units of management, and management information systems. The 1982 White Paper set out the intention of the initiative.

31

To promote in each department an organisation and system in which managers at all levels have:

a. a clear view of their objectives, and means to assess, and wherever possible measure, outputs or performance in relation to those objectives;

b. well defined responsibility for making the best use of their resources, including a critical scrutiny of output and value for money; and

c. the information (particularly about costs), the training and the access to expert advice which they need to exercise their responsibilities effectively.

(Cmnd 8616:5)

The initiative marked an important step in the devolution of financial control since an important thrust of FMI is to alter the way in which decisions are made about public expenditure and to promote accountable management. Essentially, accountable management is based on the notion of stewardship. This is a relationship in which one party (the principal), entrusts resources and responsibilities to another party (the steward) and requires her/him to give an account of the discharge of these responsibilities (Gray and Jenkins 1986). Responsibility for resources traditionally resides in the centre and responsibility for using resources is divorced from it in the hands of line managers. This has resulted in line managers seldom being given information on the cost of the resources they consume. Additionally line managers can do little to influence the resources they consume, nor do they have much control over the resources allocated to them. This separation of responsibilities is neatly summarized by Williams (1985) in relation to the Health Service when he comments: 'An unfortunate division of responsibility seems to have grown up whereby costs are the business of administrators and treasurers, while benefits are the business of doctors and nurses.'

Although the comment is directed at the Health Service it is equally apposite in the context of education. A major theme of FMI has therefore been to reunite the two responsibilities. As a result FMI has reinforced and accelerated the creation of a management role for heads and governors which gives them management responsibility for the deployment of resources supported by the necessary budgeting and cost information systems.

Local management of schools (LMS) continues these central ideas into the field of education. Within this arena the government's proposals have two main objectives:

- to ensure that parents and the community know on what basis the available resources are distributed in their area and how

much is being spent on each school;
- to give to the governors of all county and voluntary secondary schools, and of larger primary schools, freedom to take expenditure decisions which match their own priorities, and the guarantee that their own school will benefit if they achieve efficiency savings.

(DES 1987:1)

In order to secure full implementation LMS:

carries with it the requirements for an LEA to set objectives for their schools, to allocate resources to them, and then, by means of monitoring their performance, to ask schools to account for their achievements and their use of resources.

(Coopers and Lybrand 1988:5)

Delegation of managerial responsibility is one of the cornerstones of good management practice. Initially the government couched its discussions in terms of 'local financial delegation' but quickly came to realize that a successful change in the management of finance would require a broader perspective. In the first instance, it would only be successful to the extent to which it led to changes in the nature of management in schools. Second, if these changes did ensue, management practices would be affected in any case. Financial management was seen both as requiring management change and as a change agent in itself to secure the improved management of schools.

The emphasis on the managerial approach is important. In fact the switch in title from financial delegation to local management of schools confirms this wider emphasis since it implies not just economically run services, but more importantly the disposition to question existing and proposed provision as follows: What are we doing? Why are we doing it? Is it worthwhile? Are we achieving what we set out to achieve? Are we achieving it at reasonable cost? Are there alternative and cheaper ways of achieving the same result? Financial devolution should assist this managerial approach.

At the school level, it will require a shift from local administration of centrally determined programmes to local management of resources. The differences between administration and management are numerous and will, in practice, necessitate considerable change in role for staff, headteachers and governors.

In some ways, the application of the concepts of financial delegation to schools is not entirely new. To a greater or lesser extent, LEAs have for many years been giving schools the freedom to spend a proportion of the money available to them as they best see fit: for example, capitation allowance schemes covering expenditure on books and equipment have been operating for many years now. However, 1981 saw a new generation of more far-reaching schemes begin when Solihull set up a pilot scheme. The scheme comprised a comprehensive school, a sixth form college and a primary school. It devolved from the outset all items except meals, transport and loan charges. By April 1985 the scheme had been extended to eight schools in total. The Cambridgeshire scheme which is well documented is broadly similar, although it omitted premises maintenance. Set up in 1982 with one primary and six secondary schools, it extended to all secondary schools in 1987, backed by a central support team, and to a large primary pilot group. Lincolnshire set up Project Seven with seven secondary schools in 1983. It devolved items of expenditure in stages (including school meals) and made extensive use of information technology.

In other authorities the initiative is more piecemeal. For example, Somerset has extensive virement arrangements and a unified target scheme for fuel/lettings/caretaking charges. Cheshire has made all secondary schools cost centres, though so far with only limited delegation. Craig (1987), Downes (1988) and Roberts and Streatfield (1988) present a fuller discussion of these schemes. There is a general trend in most LEAs for some ad hoc delegation. LMS will, however, accelerate the process considerably.

Basic principles

The principle underlying LMS is that responsibility for the management of resources should, as far as possible, be delegated to those who use them, in this case, to schools. Delegated systems of management, including finance, are based on the claim that, if decisions about resource allocation are taken as close as possible to the operational part of the process, better quality decisions will emerge. The meaning behind the idea is that by involving people in the running of the organization, through giving them some autonomy in making their own decisions within the constraints of a predetermined budget, an incentive will be provided to improve efficiency and effectiveness. Evidence to support these claims comes from, amongst others, a 1986 report by Peat Marwick which indicates that recent evaluation studies of delegated budgetary control systems record that managers found them effective aids to resource management. The following specific benefits were cited:

- reduction in time taken to make decisions, such as whether to work overtime to deal with a peak in the workload - previously, many decisions of this type would have to be referred up the line;

- saving of staff effort at all levels because fewer decisions need to be passed up the line;
- increased awareness of costs;
- improved job satisfaction among managers.

(Peat Marwick 1986:31)

The government clearly anticipates that similar advantages will accrue to schools. Indeed evidence from the schemes already in existence and referred to above tend to support the view. Although the pilot schemes have concentrated mainly on secondary schools, the evidence from the few pilot experiments in primary schools suggests that LFM there is equally effective, although with significant differences (Stenner 1987 and 1988).

The government argues that schools will have increased incentives to seek greater efficiency and economy in their use of resources, since they will be able to use any resource savings to develop or improve their services. This is important because while efficiency and economy are laudable goals to pursue they are not sufficient motivators on their own. Effectiveness is also important. So the overriding aims of the proposed system of financial delegation are to enable the governors and headteacher of each school to make the most effective and efficient use of the resources available to them; to give schools greater flexibility and freedom within an agreed budget to spend according to local priorities; and to increase awareness within the profession of how the financial system in education operates in practice since it is important that the financial strategy supports educational aims.

The terms 'economy, efficiency, and effectiveness', referred to above, are known collectively as the three Es, and figure extensively in public management literature and discussions. Professionals within public-sector organizations including education view concepts of economy and efficiency with some suspicion, fearing that they may be incompatible with the essentially caring nature of their work. However, they form the basis of attempts to capture value-for-money measures in non-profit-orientated organizations and an understanding of them is important in that context.

Economy simply means spending or consuming as little as feasible be it minimizing the use of energy, photocopying paper or whatever. However, measures of economy do not take into account the outputs achieved in using resources. As such they have only limited usefulness as managerial tools.

Efficiency is a more complex notion than economy since it incorporates outputs as well as inputs. In fact it is normally expressed as some relationship between inputs and outputs, for example, cost per pupil. Improvements in efficiency are made possible either by increasing output while holding input constant, or by holding output constant while reducing inputs. It is important to remember, as Glynn (1987) points out, that efficiency should not be measured for efficiency's sake. Improving efficiency is the objective. Efficiency measures assist management's contribution to improving it and to determining the expected gains from suggested improvements. However, efficiency measures say nothing about the quality and value of the services provided or how they relate to policy objectives. Hence measures of effectiveness are also required: that is, ensuring that the output from any given activity is achieving the desired results. None the less, effectiveness measures are notoriously difficult to derive in practice and might in any case conflict with efficiency measures. As Hepworth (1980) observes:

> The conflict between efficiency and effectiveness, particularly in sensitive services like education and social services, is extremely difficult to resolve, and is left to individual judgments, which really means the judgment of those most concerned with the development of the service.
>
> (Hepworth 1980:239)

The important point to remember is that financial delegation and management are the means to making sound resource allocation decisions. The ends, the sound decisions themselves, will, it is hoped result in an improvement in the quality of education provided. The means should never be seen as an end in itself, otherwise a number of potential benefits from financial delegation will be lost sight of.

LMS in practice

The success or failure of delegated systems of school financial management will be crucially dependent on the attitudes of schools and their staff, the amount of professional advice and support from the LEA, and the successful implementation and operation of appropriate management information systems. CIPFA (1988) outline four criteria for the successful implementation of the schemes:

- good management training (of headteachers and governors);
- sound planning;
- good communication;
- positive attitudes.

Attitudes, however, may prove to be the most difficult obstacle to overcome in practice. If headteachers view the scheme solely as adding to their already overloaded administrative burden, with little or no reward, then the scheme will be doomed to failure. It is important in

introducing LMS to ensure that those charged with the responsibility for
its implementation view the exercise as an opportunity, which has as its
primary objective, not economies, not increased efficiency *per se*, but an
improvement in the quality of education delivered to pupils.

Resource allocation formulae

For schools there are two issues of direct relevance:

- the overall size of the school budget as determined by the LEA's
  resource allocation formula; and
- allocation of the budget in order to secure an efficient and
  effective use of available resources consistent with attainment of
  the school's objectives.

The resolution of the first issue is crucially dependent on the nature of
the resource allocation formula. The underlying basis for determining
this formula is a difficult and contentious matter. Comprehensive
discussions of the various methods by which the formula might work are
beyond the scope of this chapter. However, a few points should perhaps
be borne in mind. Whilst resource allocation formulae will need to
reflect the characteristics and priorities of each LEA, and hence there is
no single formula which can be applied, the principles underlying the
resource allocation system adopted will be instrumental in shaping the
entire scheme since it will help determine which activities can become
the school's responsibility and which must remain within the LEA.

Two alternative bases traditionally underlie the determination of
formulae. The first is based on historic levels of budgeted or actual
expenditure, the second on one or more indicators based on 'need'. In
practice, formulae adopted often combine aspects of the two alternative
approaches.

Coopers and Lybrand in their report commissioned by the DES in
May 1988 suggest that the formula should have three main components:

an amount which depends on pupil numbers, with sliding scales of
allowances, weighted by age and other factors, and with higher
rates of allocation per pupil for smaller schools; a pragmatic
allocation based primarily on the characteristics of the school's
site; limited specific allowances to reflect particular activities at
each school.

(Coopers and Lybrand 1988: 27)

The 1988 Act lays down certain rules which will govern the basis of
formulae funding by LEAs. Under LMS the LEA determines the total
resources available for the primary and secondary schools in its area.

This is known as the General Schools' Budget and it represents the amount appropriated by the LEA for any financial year in respect of all schools covered by a scheme in that year. This figure will include all direct schools' related costs, expenditure on central administration and support, and an allowance for contingency items. The mandatory and discretionary items excepted from delegation are then deducted from the General School's Budget to produce the Aggregated Schools' Budget. Mandatory excepted items include capital expenditure, specific grants, home to school transport, central administration costs and provision for inspectors/advisers. Discretionary exceptions include, for example, school meals, statemented pupils and special units and peripatetic and advisory teachers. Eventually the total cost of the items which the LEA chooses not to delegate, apart from a few exceptions, should not exceed 7 per cent of the General Schools' Budget.

The Aggregated Schools' Budget will then be allocated among schools on the basis of the Resource Allocation Formula. For the LEA as a whole, at least seventy-five per cent of the aggregated schools' budget should be allocated on the basis of numbers of pupils weighted by age. Its purpose is to ensure that the total budget available to schools is based on need criteria rather than simply perpetuating historical spending patterns. Such a basis may mean that some schools will experience difficulty in adjusting from their historical levels of funding. The formula will implicitly allocate average salary costs, but those schools with a high proportion of teachers on scale points above the average may experience a significant shortfall since schools will be charged the actual salary costs incurred. There are transitional arrangements designed to help with this problem but the transitional four-year period allowed may prove to be too short in individual cases.

Whatever the precise nature of the formula the LEA uses for allocating resources to schools, the end result will be the setting of an overall cash limit within which the schools must provide the range of services for which delegation has been agreed, the remaining services staying the responsibility of the LEA. Each school will then have to manage and plan its activities in order to achieve its educational objectives.

The budgetary control process

How can this best be achieved? In essence managing a budget involves two issues:

- Deciding the type, nature and level of activities you wish to support and therefore fund. This is the problem of determining the budget plan.

- Ensuring that this plan is implemented in practice. This is the problem of monitoring and control.

In other words, in managing its allocation from the LEA, the school will need to provide for the detailed monitoring and control of revenue expenditure to be achieved through budget holders who have the delegated responsibility for incurring expenditure within the limits authorized.

Budgetary preparation and control

As in other organizations, the key to effective budgetary control requires the preparation of a reliable opening budget. The budget must be distinguished from the LEA funding allocation outlined above. The latter is an authorization to spend money for an approved purpose. A budget, by contrast, is really a form of plan. More precisely, in the context of school financial management, a budget can be described as a statement, in financial terms, of existing activities of a school plus any proposed developments during a year less any which are now being superseded or made redundant. It enables delegation, planning, control and motivation to be achieved. As well as being a plan, a budget also acts as a control against which actual performance can be evaluated.

Anthony *et al.* (1984) list the following four characteristics of budgets:

- It is stated in monetary terms, although the monetary amounts may be backed up by non-monetary amounts (e.g. units sold or produced).
- It generally covers a period of one year.
- It contains an element of management commitment, in that managers agree to accept the responsibility for attaining the budgeted objectives.
- The budget proposal is reviewed and approved by an authority higher than the budgetee.

(Anthony *et al.* 1984:443)

Budgeting starts with a given or forecast funding allocation and seeks to divide the total resources available in a detailed breakdown between the competing activities which the organization manages. In short a budget is a costed plan with cost data providing the building-blocks with which budgets are constructed. The budget can be analysed between budget holders or a group of budget holders within a school. It should therefore be apparent that a budget can only be prepared correctly after considering the planned activities of each department for the forthcoming year. The plans must span all the activities of the school and should take into account any external constraints such as the statutory position on health and safety or any rules imposed by the LEA. Of course, planning cannot be considered in isolation from likely funding levels since it is conceivable that costed plans may exceed the available funding. In such cases, activities will have to be rethought until final agreed budgets are arrived at. This is a sensitive process which will require schools to make decisions on priorities. Agreed changes should reflect the overall objectives of the school. Across-the-board percentage reductions are therefore unlikely to reflect this.

The ultimate goal of budgeting is to assist in ensuring that an organization runs as efficiently and effectively as possible. To achieve this goal, any budgeting process involves:

- the delegation of a series of tasks and with them accountability;
- the control of performance/results.

It is crucial that budget holders should be encouraged to participate actively in budget preparation procedures as research shows that this will help to motivate them to accept specific targets and commit them to adhering to the subsequently agreed budget. Although a detailed treatment of motivational considerations is beyond the scope of this chapter, some of these aspects are mentioned below. Hofstede (1968) and Otley (1977) provide a good description of the behavioural problems associated with budget systems.

The budget should approximate to a formal model of the organization, stating its objectives, its inputs and its expected outputs. Obviously, in the field of education the question of assessing outputs causes difficulties, not least because of the difficulties in agreeing educational objectives, but the principle remains. A necessary requirement is therefore for schools to identify their objectives as a whole. The Chartered Institute of Public Finance and Accountancy (1988) lists the main areas to be covered which include:

- desired aims and character of the school;
- curriculum development and priorities;
- extra curricular activities;
- performance targets (including numbers of pupils attracted and their achievements).

At its best the budget should:

- compel the management of a school to plan ahead, to formulate targets and objectives, to identify expected levels of

performance and adopt appropriate strategies;
* provide expectations of future performance which can be used as criteria for judging actual performance;
* promote communication and co-ordination.

However, budgets need to be understood if they are to be successful. The purpose behind them and the system adopted needs to be fully appreciated by all members of staff. Although the overall purpose of the budget is to increase efficiency in the organization, different groups may use the budget for different purposes. For the politicians or the LEA the budget may be viewed as a tool to contain costs or increase efficiency. The governors, on the other hand, may view it as providing a better insight into the functioning of the school and a mechanism for improved co-operation with teachers. The headteachers may see it as a means of obtaining information about their own activities and costs, which may strengthen their position in negotiating for more resources. Finally teachers and technicians may see the budget as facilitating increased participation in management decision making, thereby giving them a chance to have more say in the running of departments.

Incremental budgeting

Basically there are two main approaches to preparing budgets: incremental budgeting and zero-based budgeting (ZBB). The incremental approach to budget preparation takes, as its starting point, the previous year's budget. Changes to the previous year's budget may be made but, by and large, these will be confined to minor changes at the margin. The vast bulk of the budget is, however, left unchanged and unchallenged, in that the budget holder is not required to justify each year the reasons for carrying out the various departmental activities and thus incurring expenditure, with the possibility and indeed likelihood, that over a period of time, any inefficiency or misuse of resources is perpetuated. To a large extent, the incremental approach to budgeting is merely a system whereby the budget for a year is little more than a roll forward from the previous year.

This approach to budgeting is one that is frequently used for a variety of reasons. First, it introduces a measure of stability into the organization. Second, it limits debate and discussion. Given that budget holders and decision makers are busy people for whom time is a scarce commodity this is an important factor. Third, budgeting is a political activity, which by its nature creates winners and losers. Incrementalism generally reflects a situation in which power in an organization is relatively diffuse, where, for example, decision making in the school is highly consensual. Avoidance of open conflict is an aspect of the culture of most schools. It is more difficult to persuade people to make radical decisions with respect to budget changes if they perceive the consequences as having an adverse impact on their activities. This is not merely self-interest. Most of us are likely to think that what we do is of value, and hence the more we do of it, the more inherently beneficial it is.

However, this approach to budgeting has a number of shortcomings. Incrementalism does not properly allow for the technical problem of the revenue consequences of capital expenditure; for example, if a school decides to purchase computers some provision should be made to cover the future cost of maintaining them. Budgeting by incrementalism tends to neglect problems that occur over a period of time. It is not sufficiently forward-looking. In addition, if the problems facing schools are changing and changing rapidly, then incrementalism is not a sensible way to attempt to budget and manage strategically.

Zero-based budgeting

It was in response to the deficiencies of the incremental approach to budget preparation that ZBB was developed, mainly in the USA. ZBB adopts a totally different approach to budget compilation. As the name implies, the budget-setting process starts at a zero base instead of the previous year's budget as under incremental budgeting. Budget holders have to justify their claims, not only for additional resources, but also for maintaining resources in existing activities. No existing budget is automatically accepted and each budget holder is, therefore, required to justify the whole of the budgetary request by indicating:

- the proposed budget for each of the proposed departmental activities for both existing and new activities;
- a valuation of the benefits accruing from each of those activities.

The next stage involves an aggregation of all the activities of the organization in an order of ranking according to the descending value of the estimated net benefits. Since the school will be subject to a cash limit and hence will not have unlimited resources at its disposal, a line will have to be drawn at the stage where the cumulative total estimated costs equals the total financial resources available. Activities below this line would either not be implemented, or if already in existence, discontinued.

It will no doubt already have been appreciated that whilst in theory the concept of ZBB appears to be an extremely efficient method of obtaining the maximum benefit from the use of resources, its practical application is fraught with difficulty.

Most of the criticisms of ZBB apply to it in its pure form, but a less complex and time-consuming form of ZBB, known as priority based budgeting (PBB) can still be usefully applied. PBB encourages staff to examine their activities and to decide on priorities thereby enabling top management to consider the activities of the school as a whole. A modified process replaces the complex valuation of benefits by a subjective assessment of priorities and all departmental activities are then listed in this order of priority, together with the individual costs of each activity. If the priorities indicated are accepted by management, those above the cut-off line are implemented or continued and those below the cut-off line are rejected; alternatively, consideration is given as to whether it is practical for those which are already in operation to be discontinued or their levels of activity reduced.

This alternative modified process does, of course, introduce the management problem of amalgamating all the departmental priority lists into one school priority list and this might be a process which is both imprecise and difficult to validate in certain circumstances. On the other hand, the actual process of determining departmental priorities could prove a highly salutary exercise and one which may be beneficial where it could form the basis of, say, a quinquennial scrutiny of each department's activities.

Monitoring and control

After the budget has been presented in summary to the governing body for consideration and approval, it remains necessary for a detailed monitoring and control mechanism to be maintained. In order to ensure that a constant scrutiny of expenditure as compared to the authorized budgets is maintained, a system of budgetary statements is provided to budget holders. These should incorporate details of actual expenditure incurred in comparison with budget. To ensure an accurate picture of the funds remaining available for spending within the budget limits, there needs to be a regular system of reporting summarized budgetary statements to governors and the LEA. The successful achievement of these aims will entail the supply of frequent, regular, timely and accurate reports to budget holders.

Budgetary control procedures are needed, not only to provide an early warning of possible overspending, but equally importantly, to identify areas where underspending is occurring. In this connection there are various formats of the types of reports usually made available to budget holders but they all essentially contain the following information:

• expenditure for the month

- budget for the month;
- variance over/under;
- total (cumulative) expenditure to date;
- budget to date;
- variance over/under.

The formal management-control system which is usually built around a financial structure provides the essential information for correcting major variations from plans. However, it must be remembered that management control includes informal as well as formal controls. Those happenings that various managers see, hear, sense and correct immediately together with formal control signals are also an integral part of the control process.

In the case of budget holders, the primary purpose of scrutiny and monitoring is to ensure that the progress of expenditure is in accord with the funds allocated, thereby indicating that the service being provided is in accord with that envisaged. For practical purposes this can be approached on two main fronts – the control of staff and non-staff expenditure.

Over 70 per cent of the school's budget is spent on employing staff and obviously this is an important area in which to exercise control. Although covering a smaller proportion of the budget than salaries and wages, the non-staff expenditure part of the budget has its own problems, particularly where the level of expenditure is directly or indirectly related to the level of pupil activity.

Perhaps one of the keys to success with this section of the budget is to identify and separate avoidable and unavoidable expenditure. In this context, avoidable refers to expenditure which can be curtailed or postponed without immediate effect on services, and it is in these categories where action would be taken in order to ensure that the ongoing level of services can be maintained without the level of unavoidable expenditure exceeding the total budget. Admittedly this can only be a temporary or transitional measure – avoidable expenditure which is continually curtailed or postponed eventually becomes firmly unavoidable.

For budgetary control to be effective it is important that individual budgets realistically reflect the expected or planned work activities/loads of departments and furthermore that such budgets are perceived as being realistic by the relevant budget holders, otherwise they will not feel committed to achieving their particular budget targets.

To give people in a department a further incentive to achieve efficiency, in addition to that from involvement in the budgeting process itself, a reward system should be introduced. Thus if a department stays within its original budget and makes savings due to increased efficiency, a percentage of that saving might be retained by the department and spent in a way the department wants. This will foster an increased awareness of the opportunity costs of their own actions and make them more ready to weigh one resource use against another.

Effective budgeting needs built-in incentives to encourage budget holders to seek planned savings, and sanctions against budget holders who underperform or who overspend without first negotiating over the need and the availability of resources. Negotiated virement and carry-forward are means of budgetary control more flexible to meet needs.

(Perrin 1988:49)

A more implicit reward is the appreciation of colleagues if the budget holder succeeds in staying within his budget. This may sound exaggerated but conversations with budget holders suggests that praise of peers can be an important incentive.

The principles of good budgeting set in an education context have been outlined. Its essential attributes are that it distributes authorization to spend money on resources, and that it monitors, reports and controls the expenditure outturn which follows. But all of this provides no clue as to managerial performance in achieving value for money. Conformity to budgets in no way gives assurance that services have been delivered economically, efficiently, or effectively. In order to monitor the latter objectives we must have relevant and accurate activity information to set beside budgetary, costing and other financial information.

Performance measurement

Accountability for performance is central to management. Yet systems for measuring and reporting performance are often regarded as problematic and controversial. There is, however, much greater scope for the quantification of output and performance in education than has been common hitherto. None the less, genuine conceptual and statistical problems need to be overcome in any attempt to undertake such measurement, but the lack of priority attached to the derivation of such measures in the past is probably the main explanation for the dearth of present measures. This is likely to change. The Department of Education and Science interest in performance indicators (Appendix B of the Coopers and Lybrand Report) and the pilot schemes in seven local authorities are all evidence of a growing concern to develop performance data which can assist parents in making better-informed choices.

It will be appreciated that designing performance measures is a particularly difficult area. A key issue is how such a system might be used. At one extreme it may be viewed simply as an information set to inform parents, governors and senior officials of what is going on in schools. Alternatively it may become an intrinsic part of the resource allocation process to make decisions on priorities. Nevertheless, sets of indicators are required to demonstrate the evidence where performance is good, or to encourage reform and improvement where performance is weak.

The main aim of education might be summarized in rather general terms as the development of the full potential of pupils. This will involve the development of basic cognitive skills such as numeracy and literacy plus the development of non-cognitive personal and social attitudes. The only readily available indicators of educational output or performance on a national basis are examination results. These indicators tell us nothing about non-cognitive achievement and it also raises questions about the relative weight to be attached to academic and non-academic educational activities. In practice, however, examination performance is regarded as important by parents, employers and pupils and in the absence of better performance measures may have some value within the management process. As Allen *et al.* argue:

> The absence of performance indicator type information, even if imperfect, could leave open a vast field of unasked and unanswered questions and give refuge to those with biased and untested opinions.
>
> (Allen *et al.* 1987:83)

Conclusion

Obviously if new financial and related management systems are to be introduced quickly and effectively, there must be a large investment in staff training. Leaving aside the issue of whether or not the investment in staff training at all levels will be either adequately funded or sharply enough focused on practical needs, there is the further problem that training will be wasted if staff are not supplied with the necessary tools. The tools in this case are the computers, the software, the additional specialist staff needed to run these systems and to advise managers and governors on how to use the output as effective information for planning resource use and taking decisions. Practice and experience should then carry the process forward. Nevertheless there still remains an enormous task in changing attitudes and in altering the culture so that the new systems and information are used to effect action, and not simply regarded as monitoring devices. Successful implementation of the scheme will require significant resources and commitment both from within the education service and from without.

Appendix 3.1

Timetable for implementation of LMS

30 September 1989	Submission of scheme for approval including a proposed timetable for phased implementation.
1 April 1990	Formula funding applies to all schools in scheme. Schools may receive delegated budgets.
1 April 1993	All qualifying schools must receive delegated budgets.
1 April 1994	Transitional arrangements end.

Note: For Inner London the years are 1991, 1992, and 1994.

References

Allen, D., Harley, M., and Makinson, G.T. (1987) 'Performance indicators in the National Health Service', *Social Policy and Administration*, vol. 21, no. 1, spring.

Anthony, R., Dearden, J., and Bedford, N. (1984) *Management Control Systems*, 5th edn, Illinois: Irwin.

CIPFA (1988) *Local Management in Schools: A Practical Guide*, London: Chameleon Press.

Coopers and Lybrand (1988) *Local Management of Schools: A Report to the Department of Education and Science*, London: HMSO.

Cmnd 8616 (1982) *Efficiency and Effectiveness in the Civil Service*, London: HMSO.

Craig, I. (ed.) (1987) *Primary Management in Action*, London: Longman.

DES (1987) *Financial Delegation to Schools: Consultation Paper*, London: HMSO.

Downes, P. (ed.) (1988) *Local Financial Management in Schools*, Oxford: Basil Blackwell.

Glynn, J.J. (1987) *Public Sector Financial Control and Accounting*, Oxford: Basil Blackwell.

Gray, A.G. and Jenkins, W.I. (1986) 'Accountable management in British central government: some reflections on the financial management initiative', *Financial Management and Accountability*, Autumn.

Hepworth, N.P. (1980) *The Finance of Local Government*, 6th edn, London: George Allen & Unwin.

Hofstede, G.H. (1968) *The Game of Budget Control*, New York: Barnes & Noble.

Otley, D.T. (1977) 'Behavioural aspects of budgeting', *Accountants Digest*, no. 49, summer.

Peat Marwick (1986) *Financial Management in the Public Sector*, Bournemouth: Bourne Press Limited.

47

Perrin, J. (1988) *Resource Management in the NHS*, Wokingham: Van Nostrand Reinhold (UK).

Roberts, B.E. and Streatfield, D. (1988) 'Local financial management systems', *International Journal of Educational Management*, vol. 2, no. 2.

Stenner, A. (1987) 'School-centred financial management', in I. Craig, (ed.) *Primary School Management in Action*, London: Longman.

Stenner, A. (1988) 'LFM in a primary school', in P. Downes (ed.) *Local Financial Management in Schools*, Oxford: Basil Blackwell.

Williams, A. (1985) 'Medical ethics: Health Service efficiency and clinical freedom', Nuffield/York Portfolio no. 2, London: Nuffield Provincial Hospitals Trust.

Chapter four

Computers in school management

Reg North

There can be little doubt that, in the changed arena mapped by the earlier chapters, education managers will become major consumers and producers of information. Even in the current situation the information requirements for managing schools are considerable, and growing rapidly with time. As the policy for the local management of schools becomes fully operative there will occur an unprecedented escalation in both quantity and complexity of information required to manage even small schools. In these circumstances education managers will understandably place a premium on having easy and quick access to high-quality information required for decision making and strategic planning activities. The message is clear: if schools are to take full advantage of their devolved powers a great deal of attention will need to be paid to information resource management.

Unlike their counterparts in industry and commerce, few education managers have received training in the techniques of information resource management. Yet, even now, schools are beginning to face the difficulties of creating a detailed information base necessary to manage effectively an institution with a financial turnover equivalent to that of a medium-sized business. Moreover, in the understandable haste to develop computer-based tools for the provision of basic financial, operational, and output information to meet the initial perceived management requirements, there is a risk that schools will undergo a technology-driven education management revolution. The risk faced is that the evolution of education management styles and processes will be largely influenced, not by an understood and debated management philosophy, but by what is perceived to be the most effective way of responding to the questions generated by the data requirements of computer software, largely influenced by current commercial applications. If the shaping of future education management styles and processes by a series of *ad hoc* responses to crises is to be avoided, managers in education will need to play an active part in the development of all aspects of information resource management.

Based on these assumptions, this chapter has been designed to meet two objectives. The first is to assist headteachers, senior management and governors in meeting their obvious and urgent need to acquire a working knowledge of computer-based management information systems so that they can operate effectively in the changed arena. The second is to provide the necessary information which will allow the teaching profession to enter effectively the technological debate currently taking place at local authority level and play an influential part in ensuring that the available technology is adapted to serve educational needs, rather than *vice versa*. The following sections are intended to inform practising education managers about computer systems in enough depth to allow them both to contribute to the development of computers in education management and to use them for their purposes. Thus the earlier parts of the chapter are mainly of a technical nature, whilst the later parts are largely concerned with the practical issues of choosing, installing, and operating a computer-based school management information system.

Information as a resource

Over a decade ago Herbert A. Simon (1977) commented that we were now entering into an information revolution and that it showed every sign of being as fundamental as the energy revolution. Events in recent years have suggested that Simon was not overstating the case. Interestingly, when viewed as a resource, information has many similarities with energy. Unlike energy, however, or any other physical resource, information resources are not consumed when they are used. This paradox of information consumption means that there are fewer constraints on its use than on other conventional resources. Although information is not a cost-free resource since its collection and distribution can be an extremely time-consuming and, therefore, expensive operation, its ability to allow reformation to suit a variety of needs is perhaps its most potent property. The challenge of effective resource management is thus to design a system which uses a common base of data capable of delivering appropriate information to meet a range of needs within the school. If this challenge is met education managers should be in a better position to exercise good judgement in school decision-making situations.

An information system

How can advantage be taken of these two resource properties of information: that information is not consumed when it is used and that it is capable of being shaped into many different forms suitable for a variety of purposes? Before considering how to build an information system within schools, some further points need to be developed. First, there is a need to construct the means by which information can be delivered to a recipient in a language and form which can be understood and which is relevant to achieving a purpose already recognized. Second, it is important to appreciate that an information system is really a subsystem of the organization, and should be designed to function in a way that serves the objectives of the school. This is not a semantic distinction but a crucial point to bear in mind when designing the information (sub)system for schools. It is all too easy for technology to lead management reform without full consideration being taken of its effects on current management practices and on the ethos of the institution. Even at a purely functional level this point has relevance for the design of information systems within schools. Enough experience of information system failure has been gained in industry and commerce to appreciate the importance of ensuring close co-operation between the system designers and its users when creating an information system. To be successful an information system should be designed so that it is compatible with the organizational and behavioural characteristics of an institution, in addition to meeting its operational demands.

The information subsystem of an organization, whether or not it is computerized, has an important function to perform in aiding management to plan, control, and operate the various subsystems of the organization in a way which assists the school to achieve its purposes. In the jargon of the art, the information subsystem is an important instrument for increasing the synergy of the organization. In other words, the information system can play an important part in pulling together the various parts of the school organization to achieve an output greater than the sum of its parts acting independently. It is recognized that although schools differ in many significant ways from organizations in industry and commerce there are clear similarities in some of their functions. As schools enter a more commercially orientated educational world, lessons can be learnt from experiences in other sectors which can help to identify the management information requirements of schools.

The delivery of information

Careful attention needs to be given to the issue of equipment selection for the delivery of information to various parts of the education system. In assessing information-delivery needs one should attempt to project the school organization requirements as far as possible into the future. Such forecasting exercises are naturally difficult, particularly in a rapidly changing world where computer developments and demands on schools for information are difficult to predict with a high degree of certainty. Nevertheless, it is possible to make some reasonable estimates of future school information requirements that will allow effective decisions to be taken on the design and specification of a computer-based delivery system.

First, there will be increasing demands to provide support for the school administration in areas like financial management and word processing. This will require computer equipment of the kind to be found in most commercial concerns which have moved towards the 'electronic office'. Second, expansion in the educational information requirements of the school in areas such as record keeping will be greatly assisted by an appropriate computer system. Schools are already finding that recently introduced initiatives – for example, pupil profiling – require more sophisticated support systems. Third, there will occur an increasing need to communicate with the local authority which will require the installation of a computer-based electronic network capable of both sending and receiving financial, statistical, and textual information.

It is useful to consider computer-based information system equipment requirements within the two standard broad categories of hardware, the electro-mechanical components and devices which make up a computer system, and software, the set of programs which operate the computer system.

Hardware

The construction of a micro-computer system requires four sets of standard compatible components to be electronically linked together, namely a central processing unit, output devices, input devices and backing store.

The central processing unit (CPU)

The central processing unit is the heart of the computer and controls the processing of programs and data as well as managing the work carried out by peripherals, such as printers. It also contains the computer's working memory (RAM) which is used whilst data and programs are being processed. The working memory size of the computer is an important factor to consider when deciding which computer system to purchase. If the memory size is too small the computer will be limited in the kinds of program it can use and this will consequently affect the range of tasks it can carry out for the school. A suitable memory size for school administration tasks would be 625K bytes.

The input device

Some means are needed by which data can be input to the computer. The most common input device is the 'keyboard'. The layout of the keys uses the QWERTY configuration found on any typewriter, but with some extra keys to allow additional editing tasks to be carried out. It is worth mentioning at this point that accuracy in using the keyboard is vital for ensuring the integrity of the information provided by the computer system. Although many computer programs go some way towards checking the data input for correctness, such as querying the input of a pupil's age of 25 years, there is an old but none the less true saying in the computer world of 'Garbage in, garbage out'.

The output device

Once the data is processed by the computer, devices are required to communicate the information. Two devices are widely used in school information systems: a visual display unit (VDU) and a printer.

The visual display unit (VDU) operates on the same principle as a television screen, providing what is called a soft copy of current information held in the computer. This on-screen information is provided almost instantaneously, although it cannot be retained as a permanent record. Visual display units can be colour or monochrome, the latter being cheaper. Only if you expect to be using graphical displays is it worthwhile investing in a colour monitor. The most important consideration to bear in mind when stating the specifications of a VDU is the degree of resolution offered. The higher the resolution the better the quality of the screen image. For all school administration environments a high resolution VDU should be purchased to avoid eye strain when carrying out detailed work such as wordprocessing or spreadsheet operations.

Printers are required to provide a hardcopy or print-out of the computer output. There are three basic types of printer appropriate for school administration. The first is a dot-matrix printer, which uses pins to make dot patterns to form characters. Such printers are fast, relatively inexpensive and versatile, and capable of producing diagrams as well as text. The quality of the characters produced is mainly dependent upon the number of pins contained in the printer head. Cheaper dot-matrix printers containing only nine pins are not suitable for school administration operations, except for producing draft copies of documents. Schools should aim to purchase a recent dot-matrix model which uses 24 pins and is capable of producing near letter quality (NLQ) characters suitable for letters and reports. Another type of printer uses a daisywheel, producing characters in a manner similar to an electric typewriter. Although capable of producing high-quality printouts, such printers are relatively slow, expensive and noisy and are restricted to producing text. A third type of printer is the laser printer which is capable of producing extremely high quality output, similar to that found in publishing. These printers are fast and flexible but relatively expensive to purchase, operate and maintain, although costs are decreasing rapidly with time.

The backing store

All computers require the means of permanently storing information such as letters, frequently used programs and school records. The random access memory is unsuitable for this purpose as data held in RAM is lost once power to the computer is switched off or new programs and data are loaded for processing. For permanent storage of data two kinds of backing store are required: a hard disk and a floppy disk. Both devices store data on a magnetic surface, and read the data rather like a record player picking up sound from a record by moving a head across the tracks of a spinning surface. When operating the computer the hard disk acts as the main backing store and should have a capacity of at least 50 megabytes. (10 megabytes is just over 10 million characters, approximately 8,000 pages of single spaced A4 typing.) The floppy disk is a smaller, flexible disk which can be used as secondary backing store by making back-up copies of all important data and programs. These back-up copies can be stored in a secure environment and used to reconstruct the information system if data is lost from the hard disk through a technical malfunction. It is crucial to ensure that back-up copies of data are systematically made of the data stored on the hard disk. Always operate on the assumption that something will go wrong with the system and that reconstruction of the information held on the hard disk will need to be carried out. Unless these simple but important good housekeeping procedures are followed, the school could find itself in a most difficult position in the event of a system failure.

Floppy disks can also be used to carry data in magnetic form through the letter post, although it is important to ensure that they are adequately protected from being damaged during transit. This allows the school to send essential information to the local authority in a form which is immediately available for processing. For example, monthly updates on financial expenditures made by the school can be sent to the local education authority. With floppy disks having an average storage capacity equivalent to 200 pages of A4, it is possible to send substantial quantities of data through the post relatively quickly and at low cost.

It may also be possible for a school to transfer data electronically to a local authority computer through the British Telecom phone system. To make this electronic link an additional piece of hardware called a modem needs to be plugged into the school computer. The modem simply converts the electronic signals which are used to operate the computer into audio signals for transmission along the telephone network. The link is made by dialling the telephone number of the local authority computer. Once this connection is made data can be automatically transferred by the computer software. The capacity to transfer information by this means opens many communication possibilities under the broad title of electronic mail. Indeed a great deal of the information which is currently sent through the postal service can already be transmitted through an electronic mail system.

Software

Without a comprehensive set of instructions in the form of a program the computer will remain an inert potential resource. The selection of well proven, easy to use software is essential for the provision of an effective computer-based school information system. There are two broad categories of software that are of significance to school computer-based information systems, namely, operating system software and applications software.

Operating system software

Computer systems are complex arrangements of electro-mechanical components which need to be managed in a way that ensures minimum human intervention and maximum automation. This computer management function is the role played by operating system software. Knowledge of the type of operating system used by a computer is essential for those making judgements about which computer system to adopt within the school, although knowledge about how an operating system works is not important. It is sufficient to appreciate that the adoption of a computer which uses a given operating system will determine the kinds of application program that can be used to support school administration.

The field is changing rapidly and an operating system advocated one year may well be superseded in the next. The best advice that can be offered is first to select the applications software that appears to be the most appropriate to the school's particular administration needs, then select the computer system. The important point to bear in mind is that the operating system is built into the computer and will thus determine the kind of applications software that it can operate, although some computers may run two operating systems thereby allowing a wider range of applications software to be adopted for the school.

Applications software

Computer systems can carry out a range of operations applicable to school administration, many of which have been well tested in commercial situations similar to those found in educational environments. Three of the most useful applications packages are wordprocessing, spreadsheets and databases.

Wordprocessing software once loaded on to the hard disk allows the computer to carry out functions that were previously in the domain of the typewriter. Instead of typing characters directly on to paper, the word processing software displays the 'typed' characters on the VDU screen and, at the same time, stores the document in its working random access memory. The document stored in the working memory can be transferred to the hard disk backing store from which it can be retrieved at a later date and published on the attached printer. The process is identical to typing except that the characters appear on the VDU screen rather than on paper. This allows corrections to be carried out electronically – no need any longer for messy correction fluid.

The major advantage offered by the wordprocessor is that documents can be amended without retyping the whole text. Another advantage of wordprocessing is that it allows documents to be produced which are neat and consistent with both left- and right-hand margins justified, pages automatically numbered, headings centred and boldly printed, sections indented or highlighted and spelling automatically validated. When a laser printer is used it is possible to avoid typesetting, thereby allowing the school magazine, for example, to be printed directly by a publisher working from a camera-ready copy.

Apart from producing a better product the wordprocessor can achieve considerable savings in secretarial cost through the efficiencies it offers. In addition to typist time saved by easy modification of documents, time can be saved by storing a range of standard letters on the backing store which can be called up into the working memory for particular details to be included. Thus letters to parents or retailers, which frequently have many standard phrases and formats, can be produced rapidly.

Spreadsheets are powerful pieces of software which can greatly facilitate budgeting decision-making processes as well as provide a comprehensive picture of a school's financial position. A spreadsheet is designed to produce a two-dimensional matrix, with a horizontal axis graded by letters and a vertical axis graded in numbers. This arrangement produces a grid, with each 'box' in the grid identified by reference to a letter (column) and number (row). The effect produced is similar to that of a large sheet of paper divided into squares. A particular square would be identified by its coordinates such as D,17. In each of the boxes it is possible to place either a numerical value or a label or a formula which defines a relationship between a number of boxes in the matrix. It is this last element, the use of personally constructed formulae, which makes the spreadsheet such a powerful financial planning tool.

Once the accounting table is constructed using the formula option to connect numerical variables, any changes in the data are automatically carried through the whole table, including adjusting subtotals and totals. This ability of the spreadsheet to recalculate the whole table in response to a change in one or more of the variables makes the possibility of asking quite complex 'What if. . .?' questions during planning meetings a realistic option for school managers. In the changed arena the ability to see at once the overall financial consequences of a particular decision on the school can be a valuable asset to strategic planning. Using a well constructed spreadsheet it should be possible to obtain rapidly an answer to such questions as '*What* would be the effect on our budget *if* teachers X,Y, and Z attended a specific in-service programme?' or '*What* would happen to the school's library purchasing ability *if* we transferred 7 per cent of our small equipment budget?'

Database software is the core of a computer-based management information system. The concept of a database is not easily described. Perhaps the best way forward is to relate it to the familiar existing paper-based administrative systems found in all schools. A school may well have its collection of data on pupils on different record cards. In some cases these cards may well be held in separate locations. There will be a pupil record containing personal information such as home address, contact telephone numbers, school from which transferred and important medical details. There will exist an academic record as well as a record of personal achievement, and so on. As much of the data contained on these record cards is identical there will be repetition of data. A change of address or form group or teacher will entail amending a number of record cards. This is not only a time-consuming task but also one which can lead to errors if not attentively and systematically carried out. Apart from containing data on pupils, the record cards themselves are used to generate data, such as class lists, option groups, mailing lists, and LEA statistical returns. In addition to pupil records there are also teacher records required for a number of different purposes.

The work of the school can be greatly facilitated by the construction of a single computer database designed to contain a collection of inter-related data stored together and capable of serving a number of applications. This is achieved by storing on a hard disk all the data which are currently held on a number of record cards but extracting only that information which the user requires. In other words there will exist only one common pool of data held on the computer to provide infor-mation for a wide range of management requirements. For example, there will be only one record for each pupil, but it will contain all relevant data for that pupil. This same single block of pupil data would be used by, say, the school secretary wishing to produce a pre-printed address for an envelope, the school timetabler producing an option list or the headteacher requesting a profile of a particular pupil's results.

A key feature which makes the database a powerful management tool is its ability to search rapidly through the data and produce information which fits the user's defined conditions. This search is carried out by using the database query language which is a part of the database management system. The query language comes as an integral part of the package and allows the user to construct questions in everyday language for the purposes of interrogating the database. For example, it might be useful in certain circumstances to know which pupils live in a specific street. To retrieve the required information the database query language could be used to ask the necessary question by giving the computer the statement STREET CONTAINING 'WEST'. The rapid response from the computer is to display on the VDU a list of all pupils who lived in West Street. The query language of the database system can cope with quite lengthy requests for information through the user coupling statements with OR and/or AND links. For example, we could extend our search for a specific group of pupils responding to query MEDICAL HISTORY CONTAINING 'DIABETIC' AND IN FORM CONTAINING '2F'. In response to this query the computer outputs a list of all those students in Form 2F who are registered as diabetics. More than two parameters can be built into a query by using a combination of OR and AND connections and following a set of rules based on Boolean logic.

The administrative power offered by well constructed database software is likely to seduce school management into a state of database dependency. There is nothing wrong in abandoning a paper-based system in favour of an electronic system providing certain data security safeguards are taken. Indeed, it would be most inefficient to operate two management information systems. The need to ensure that effective arrangements are made to back up data stored on the hard disk has already been pointed out. However, in addition to these arrangements a data protection system should also be included as a part of the database management system purchased for the school.

Data security is, in effect, achieved by the database software itself in two ways. First, by having a system of passwords which must be input to the computer before the user can gain access to the database, it is possible to allocate priorities to ensure that the user can only access that data to which he or she is entitled. For example, the system could be designed in a way that allows only the headteacher's password to gain access to staff data. Second, data can be protected through the password system by allowing only one person the authority actually to write data into the system, although many may be given the authority to read data. Although passwords offer the school a degree of data security which can be enhanced by an effective system of physical security, protecting valuable data from damage, wilful or accidental, will always remain an area for concern.

A carefully constructed database will provide several advantages. Above all, access to the information will be rapid, and should allow automatic and flexible report generation. The data itself will be consistent, easier to check and amend, and more up-to-date. With suitable safeguards and the use of controlled access, privacy and security can also be improved.

Setting up an information system

The introduction of a computer-based school administration system is a complex management task requiring careful planning and sensitivity to natural fears that some office staff may have in adapting to the initial complexities of a new technology. The key point to bear in mind when setting up a computer-based school administration system is that conversion from the existing paper-based arrangements should be taken slowly, one step at a time. However, it is crucial that each step is systematically related to the intended final state. In other words, it is advisable to take a modular approach, but to ensure that each module is compatible with both the hardware and other modules. The intention should be eventually to achieve a fully integrated system so that, for example, the database adopted can be used by wordprocessing software. To achieve a fully integrated system, which may take three or four years, it is advisable for school managers to move through a number of interrelated development stages.

Setting system objectives

A clear statement of the functional objectives the computer-based information is expected to meet is an essential first step in the development process and requires management to engage in effective consultation procedures with staff. A number of objectives for a school's computer-based information system could be cited, although specific individual requirements may be added. In general, the main functional objectives of a computer-based information system should be to:

- reduce time required to provide letters, reports, and documents by using wordprocessing;
- offer a single database of pupil information capable of producing information in a range of standard formats and responding to specific search requests;
- produce standard statistical reports requested by the local authority;

59

- provide the means of analysing, controlling, and auditing all
  financial transactions;
- aid the school timetabling process and extract statistical
  information from timetables;
- offer a single database of staff details with the capability of
  extracting essential information as required.

Identifying user requirements

This stage in the developmental process should involve the staff in a
detailed identification of the school's information technology needs. A
fairly standard approach would cover the following areas:

Wordprocessing

Once the system is installed it is quite likely that the wordprocessing
facilities will be first and most frequently used. Indeed, it is good
psychology to install the wordprocessing module first as its
cost-effectiveness will be quickly realized by the office staff. There are
a number of wordprocessing packages on the market from which to
choose. When making a decision on which package to purchase three
points should be borne in mind. First, is the package easy to use and
supported by a training programme? Second, does it have the facility to
retrieve data from other parts of the system, such as financial tables from
the financial package or parents' names and addresses from the pupil
record system? In other words can it be 'integrated' with the whole
system? Third, does it contain all the standard features that are generally
required to support a high-quality commercial organization?

Pupil requirements

The software needed to support the administrative requirements of
pupils is extensive and quite complex. The first issue to be decided is the
range of purposes which the software must satisfy since only then is it
possible to state the data items which must be stored on the database.
However, it is worth remembering that as the school gains experience in
using the system and fully appreciates its potential, new information
outputs are likely to be demanded. Thus any system which is purchased
should have room for expansion.

It is useful to begin, as it were, at the end and consider the output
requirements for pupil administration. We might consider the large
number of lists schools make of pupils, usually in alphabetical order:
form groups, option subject choice, examination mark lists, bus passes
and so on. A second area of administrative concern is the requirement to
produce pupil profiles and end-of-term reports. Coupled with this aspect
is the need in secondary schools and tertiary colleges to respond to

requests for references from prospective employers. Many of these requests have the unhappy knack of arriving a number of years after a pupil has left the school or during the summer holiday period. There is also a number of requirements to produce statistical returns, like the DES Form 7 age breakdown return. The requirement under the Education Reform Act to test pupil attainment at 7, 11, 14, and 16 will also necessitate careful compilation of data which can be easily retrieved. Any computer-based system must be able to produce outputs that will provide the necessary information to support these and other administrative requirements.

Once the output requirements have been identified it is a relatively easy task to state the data needs. For each pupil, a record will be created which contains all individual data items. Each data item is contained separately in an area called a 'field'. Typically a database will allow any individual record to contain up to 40 fields. Thus it is possible to create a pupil record which contains 40 pieces of data which may be retrieved in part or together by a database management system. It is common practice to nominate one of the fields as a key field to ensure unique pupil identification. (By allocating to each pupil a number, confusion is avoided in searching for John Smith, for example.) There are some common fields that will need to be created to meet individual school requirements, such as pupil name, address, date of birth, telephone number, parents' names, form group, medical history, primary school attended, subject choices, teacher assessments, school examination marks, attainment test records, GCSE results, absences from school.

Financial requirements

The information requirements generated by the demands of local financial management of schools present a new problem for the education system. However, financial-control software systems, which use universal principles and techniques, have been successfully used in the commercial world for a number of years. This is not to suggest that there are no difficulties in developing effective financial software to meet the specific demands of schools. However, we are in a position to identify information requirements based on experiences culled from commercial enterprises.

The main objective of a computer-based financial system should be to assist the school to achieve a high degree of accuracy and control over its financial transactions with a minimum of clerical work. To achieve this objective, financial software should cover the areas of budgeting control, purchasing orders, and inventories, and should provide an analysis at various organizational levels.

Budgeting control. In the new era it will be essential for headteachers to have an accurate up-to-date picture of school expenditure in a form which will allow an overall school view as well as a detailed breakdown of individual departmental expenditures and commitments. The information provided by the system should therefore ensure that the headteacher is in a position to monitor effectively expenditure against budgets and compare the value of requisitions with allocated budgets throughout the school. The system should also be capable of producing accounts in a format which is compatible with LEA requirements.

Purchasing orders. The software required for purchases made by the school should allow all requisitions and receipts to be monitored with the minimum of clerical work. It should accommodate all purchases in areas such as heating fuel, capital items, maintenance, books, and equipment.

Inventory control. Within the financial package there should be the facility to provide an up-to-date inventory of all equipment held by the school. Once the inventory has been constructed and stored on the database any subsequent purchases made and monitored by the purchase order software are easily transferred to the inventory.

In addition to the above standard financial packages schools may well use the opportunity offered by the new facility to convert their existing school fund holdings and imprest accounts into computer-based accounts.

Statistical returns

Other areas of the education system have information needs too, and make demands of schools to supply data on a range of topics. Some of these requests for school data are required on an annual or monthly basis and are given in a standard format. Other requests are 'one-offs' whose data demands are difficult to predict. Nevertheless, in each case a computer-based information system should be able to produce statistical returns by extracting the required data from the existing database and using the modules already installed. The statistical software should therefore be capable of extracting data from pupil and teacher records, financial applications and timetabling applications, and compiling them into an approved format.

Staffing requirements

It is essential for school managers to have up-to-date information about the teaching and non-teaching personnel. However, experience has shown this to be a particularly sensitive area in computer-based information systems. Nevertheless, there are a number of advantages in creating a staff database. First, it can be used to extract statistical information required by the LEA and the DES. Second, it can play a valuable role in providing information for staff development programmes, including a record of individual in-service expenditure which the school must meet under the proposed financial arrangements. Third, comprehensive details of staff qualifications and experience would be of value when constructing the school timetable. In addition to current teaching staff, the database should also include comprehensive details of teachers in the area able to act as substitute teachers. Using the search facilities available through the database management system, it would be quite easy to quickly retrieve details of suitable substitutes to cover absent teachers.

Timetabling and curriculum analysis

A number of software packages have been developed over the last ten years to assist with the construction of the school timetable. Most school timetablers, however, still appear to prefer their own methods, claiming that the computer-based solutions do not adequately handle many of the idiosyncratic constraints and procedures found in their particular school. There is in schools a lack of knowledge about timetabling software rather than a shortage of useful programs. The situation is changing quickly and a number of schools are reporting the availability of much improved timetabling software and claim to receive assistance through its use. Notwithstanding the ambiguous situation with regard to complete timetabling software, there are useful computer-based timetabling support systems available which are able to use the existing pupil and staff databases to provide option scheduling, course planning assistance, and curriculum analysis.

In addition to producing, analysing and costing a school's curriculum provision, a number of effective software packages exist which uses the pupil database to produce external examination entries and a subsequent analysis of the results.

Software selection

This is arguably the most important decision that will be made in the developmental process. There are two possible routes that can be taken. The first route takes the school down the path of commissioning its own software, either by in-house development or by employing a programmer to produce software tailored to meet the specific needs of the school. Although there are obvious advantages in having individually designed software, the cost of the exercise is usually prohibitive for a single school.

The more advisable route to take is to examine existing software packages and select the one which best appears to fit a school's individual requirements. There are a number of companies specializing in educational administration software in the United Kingdom.

When deciding on a school administration package a number of points should be considered. Assuming that no commitment has yet been made towards the hardware, the following selection criteria can be used in the decision making process:

- Does the system follow a modular approach, thereby allowing the information base to grow gradually in tune with the school's own developmental pace?
- Is there a common database from which all other applications can extract their information requirements?
- Is the system flexible enough to allow a school's special requirements to be facilitated?
- Is the system fully integrated with other components, such as the wordprocessor and financial packages?
- Will the software house maintain the packages once they are installed and incorporate any future changes arising from government legislation?
- Is the cost of the whole package, including training and hardware requirements, competitive?
- Is training given to key personnel?
- Does it incorporate a sophisticated data security system?
- Will the system be supported by the local authority?

This last point could well be the deciding factor in the software selection process as many local education authorities may well have made a commitment to purchase under licence a software package for their schools. Nevertheless, there are strong arguments for the practitioners of the administrative systems to join the debate and satisfy themselves that the right decision has been made.

Hardware selection

Once the software has been selected it is only then possible to select the hardware for the school-based management information system. It is quite probable that financial considerations will be a major factor in the decision-making process, although software specifications will define the kind of operating system, random access memory size, hard-disk backing store capacity and printer type that is required for successful operation of the package.

It is, however, unlikely that a single stand-alone computer will adequately meet the management information needs of an average-sized secondary school. Bearing this in mind it is prudent to ensure that it is possible to build additional computers into the system when funds become available at a future date as a decision will eventually need to be made on whether or not to build a network of three or four computers or have stand-alone machines. This is not an easy decision to take. The major advantages of a network are that it allows the computers to use the same peripherals and software and to share data. Major disadvantages are that the whole system may become inoperative if one component fails, delays may be encountered whilst waiting for the printer, and there may be a lower level of security for data held on the system. This last point is possibly the one of greatest concern for a school information system where security and integrity of data are of great importance. If a networked system is installed it is important to build into the network a series of priority passwords which restrict access to sensitive data items and prevents unauthorized additions or deletions being made to the databank.

Becoming operational

Once the system is installed the school can begin to convert its existing operations and procedures to a computer-based system. It will be the task of management to decide on its priorities for computer-based support and delegate responsibilities for action. It should be anticipated that a number of early problems will be likely to cause frustration and dissatisfaction with the new system. This is only to be expected when even the most trivial misunderstandings, such as omitting to switch on a part of the system, will present difficulties, particularly if the office staff are operating under the pressures of a normal school day.

It is vital for the successful implementation of computer-based management information to establish an overall strategy in which scheduling and preparation are key tactical concepts.

Scheduling

It is essential when introducing a computer system into an organization with its existing demands and procedures to ensure that the hardware and accompanying software are made available at the correct time and in an order which is compatible with the school's administrative needs.

Fortunately, school life has a fairly predictable rhythm which allows the following schedule to be adopted once the hardware and software have been purchased:

- Install a word processing facility at the beginning of the Easter holiday period. This will allow the office staff time to gain experience of the system in a way which will be beneficial to the school. Two days' training should allow an experienced typist to become operational.
- During the summer holiday period the pupil record system could be created on the database, allowing form groups to be listed in

time for the beginning of the first term in September.
- During this first term, provided the pupil records have been created, the statistical return package could be used for external returns required from January onwards.
- During the second term the options package and external examination package could be evaluated by comparing the solution obtained by using the computer with the school's traditional methods.
- During the third term work could begin with the pupil profiling system in preparation for fully converting the method used by the school for assessing records of pupil achievement in time to produce reports in twelve months. A lengthy period of planning time should be given to this aspect of the computer-based management system because it is quite likely that the school will wish to modify the alternative statement options given by the software and create its own pupil comments.
- The second long vacation period is a good time to complete the database by adding staff records and creating the substitute teacher file. In addition, the external examination results analysis using the trial data inserted during the second term could be carried out and results compared with manual arrangements.
- By this time the school would have had over one year's experience of using the system, and during the next term the timetable module could be introduced and evaluated against the school's requirements.
- By the end of the next term, when the system should have been in operation for two years, it should be capable of producing the school's own version of its pupil profiles.

It will be noted that no reference has been made to the introduction of the financial software. Although the financial package will eventually need to be integrated within the whole system, there is no reason why it cannot be initially developed independently of the packages described above. Indeed, given the urgency for financial control and budgeting, it is recommended that an independent course of developmental action is taken by the senior member of staff responsible for this area. There may, however, be a problem in not being able to gain sufficient computer access to carry out the task of building a computer-based financial control system if the schedule outlined above for the administrative system is adopted, and some adjustments might be required. Each school will need to work out its own implementation programme and the schedule outlined above, offered simply as a guide, may be carried out over a shorter time period.

Preparation

Preparing for the various phases of the computer-based information is an important aspect in becoming operational and considerable benefits can be gained by paying attention to the following areas:

- The school office must be adequately prepared to accommodate the new technology. This will require a specialist working area to be created in which the correct computer furniture is provided to house the computer and printer and give secure storage facilities for disks, instruction manuals, and paper supplies. In order to maintain a quiet office environment it is advisable to enclose the dot-matrix printer in an acoustic hood.
- The reorganization of the school office to create the new space for the computer equipment can frequently cause difficulties. In part, these are due to the inadequacy of space that already exists in most school offices. In part, too, these difficulties are due to the disruption caused to the office routine and perhaps resultant loss of territory.
- Office procedures will need to be revised after a detailed analysis is carried out on responsibilities and organization to ensure that the most effective use is made of clerical time during the difficult transition period. It is, of course, important to involve the clerical staff in all discussions and decisions relating to the introduction and operation of the new technologies.
- Data collection methods and means by which data is presented for input to the computer system will require detailed analysis. In most administrative areas there will not be a need to generate new data but the means by which it is collected will need to be reappraised. In most cases the current forms which are completed by pupils, parents, and staff will need to be redesigned so that the data which are contained can be easily transferred to the computer system.

Data Protection Act

There are a number of important regulations governing the use of data held on a computer system. It is advisable that a copy of these regulations is obtained prior to installation of the system. The Data Protection Act 1984 regulates the use of automatically-processed information about individuals which is held on computers and will apply to a school's computer-based management information system. The Act requires all personal data to be registered with the Data Protection Registrar and used only in accordance with the terms under which it is registered. The Act also, importantly, requires that the data are held securely. This requires the school to ensure security of data at three levels:

- Physical security: prevention of unauthorized access to the computer and disks.
- Software security: prevention of unauthorized access to the database by way of passwords which should be frequently changed.
- Operational security: setting-up procedures concerning the disposal of computer printouts.

Under the act a 'data subject' has the right of access to personal data held in machine readable form.

Conclusion

The introduction of a computer-based management information system properly prepared for can give great benefits to the school. In addition to paying attention to good housekeeping practices, senior management should also prepare for the introduction of the system by reassessing its current organizational arrangements, particularly those related to school planning and decision-making. One of the consequences of introducing an information system is that it is likely to encourage change in existing relationships within the school. When coupled with changes emanating from the Education Reform Act, education management practices within the school organization are likely to alter significantly. A senior management team which anticipates these changes will be in a position to take full advantage of the opportunities presented by the changed arena.

References

Data Protection Act (1984), London: HMSO.
Simon, H.A.(1977) *The New Science of Management Decisions*, New York: Prentice-Hall.

Further reading

Bentley, T.(1981) *Management Information Systems and Data Processing*, London: Holt, Rinehart, and Winston.
Best, D.P.(1988) 'The future of information management', *International Journal of Information Management*, 8: 13–24.
Bird, P. (1986) *Microcomputers in School Administration*, London: Hutchinson.

Crowe, T. and Avision, D.E.(1984) *Management Information from Data Bases*, London: Macmillan.
North, R.F.J.(1988) 'Restricted choice in the management of change' *Educational Management and Administration*, 16: 163–171.

Chapter five

Marketing the school

Ernie Cave and Dave Demick

Marketing has undoubtedly entered the language and practice of education in the 1980s, but the concept is unclear, ambiguous, and much misunderstood. On the one hand there is the commonly held popular view of marketing that it has to do with expert packaging, advertising, and hard selling in the face of competition. Professionals engaged in marketing, and theorists who write about the subject, have a broader and more complex point of view. Kotler and Fox (1985), for example, who have studied the issue of marketing in non-profit-making organizations, define marketing as 'the analysis, planning, implementation and control of carefully formulated programs designed to bring about voluntary exchanges of value with target markets to achieve institutional objectives'.

Such a definition requires analysis and interpretation and may at first appear to be of little help to the harassed headteacher in the period following the passing of the Education Reform Act of 1988. Nevertheless, it is the argument of this chapter that recipes based on the narrower view of marketing will be of limited value to schools, especially in the longer run. While survival may be the bottom line for any institution, schools, surely, are pursuing multiple objectives for a wide variety of interests and it is in this context that schools can and should address marketing issues. The purpose in this chapter is to introduce important concepts applicable to such a task, and to enable school staff and governors to develop a structure around which to plan and implement their marketing activities.

Marketing is not a subject which has received much attention in the literature of education prior to the 1980s. Marketing was considered unprofessional and the idea that schools were in the business of selling a product was widely rejected. It is not a topic which has appeared on the education management courses which proliferated in the 1960s and 1970s. 'Marketing the school' rarely showed as an item on the agenda of the various working parties which came to be accepted as essential elements of school structures as the concept of management took root.

Few schools had marketing as part of the job description of a member of staff. It was, of course, easy to hold the view that marketing was only for the private sector and that schools should not be in the business of selling. Although the 1944 Act allowed the possibility of parental choice of school it was, in practice, difficult for parents to exercise that choice. Quotas and designated intake areas were determined by local education authorities, and schools were unable to enrol pupils from outside their designated areas except in exceptional circumstances.

Marketing as competition

The position is dramatically changed with the passing of the 1988 Education Reform Act. A central tenet of government policy is that extension of consumer choice in the public sector will lead to improved quality and this is reflected in the declared determination to open education to the competitive forces of the market-place. This emphasis on competition between schools may lead them to establish the recruitment of pupils as a first priority. A perception of competition as a threat to survival will reinforce a concept of marketing as merely advertising. It may come to be seen as mainly, rather than marginally, about glossy brochures, publicity for specially highlighted happenings, concentration on purely image-building events, and the like. Most teachers are aware of the dangers in all this. Russell (1988) quite properly stresses the desirability of schools establishing good working relationships with the media, especially local newspapers, and presents a useful 'press action checklist'. There is no doubt that what the papers say may assume paramount importance and she asks: how many hours of teacher time are spent nationally preparing pupils for photo-opportunities? There is an almost inevitable temptation to focus attention on the exceptional rather than on the generality of school life.

Fortunately it does not have to be like that. It is true that the extension of freedom of parental choice in the 1988 Act has been accompanied by pronouncements that the operation of free market forces will ensure that good schools will prosper and bad schools will be forced out of the market. Sadly, the theme has been taken up within the profession and terms like merchandise, product, marketing and customer are bandied without a clear analysis of their possible meaning within education. A prevailing message is that failure by the school to market its educational merchandise could mean the difference between survival and extinction. Threats to survival do not always concentrate the mind. Sometimes they disturb its good judgment and some schools may be tempted to adopt a 'hard sell' approach aimed simply at attracting pupils. Such schools might consider a number of questions.

Is the school really under threat?

Available evidence suggests that the government's apparent perception of large numbers of parents moving their children about in search of quality of education is mistaken. Certainly parents, given a choice, will move their children from a school which they perceive as bad and will seek admission to a school which they perceive as good. However, the point was made in Chapter 1 that most parents are satisfied with the school their children attend and only a small proportion of parents are likely to change schools given the opportunity. Also, where the quality of education given to the children is, in fact, poor, parents are unlikely to be fooled by a 'logo image' approach.

If the school is under real threat, can an aggressive marketing strategy change things?

Undoubtedly, in a situation where there is a declining school population, some schools will close and it is the government's intention that market forces, rather than planned rationalization, will determine which they will be. In declining areas or where pupil numbers are marginally viable, a movement away of even a few pupils can place a school under threat. However, there is no evidence to date to suggest that schools which have been forced to close or amalgamate because of declining enrolments have been ineffective either in the quality of education provided or in marketing their wares. One proposition that can be put forward from experience in Northern Ireland is that, since it has invariably been schools in socially deprived areas which have closed, the criteria for choice may be social rather than educational. Schools genuinely under threat need to determine what factors are causing the decline in numbers and which of these can be brought within the school's control. A broader marketing strategy may be required.

What are the costs of competitive marketing?

Schools have limited resources of time and energy. The school-produced magazine put out cheaply and frequently and featuring the work of a wide range of pupil ability could become less important than the expensive quality publication containing only the impressive work of the high-fliers. Open days could become 'show days' which do not reflect properly the real life of the school. The overriding importance of good examination results could dictate school policy on pupil grouping and teacher allocation to classes. If marketing is seen merely as a means of attracting a larger intake in order to avoid a threat of closure, real or imaginary, schools could become engaged in competition at the periphery of education. In this approach the core of what the school does is, at best, unaffected but may well become distorted. A final but important point: if the school is going to claim credit publicly for the pupils who go on to university, is it going to acknowledge publicly its blame for those who end up in jail?

Marketing as co-operation

The starting point of a constructive, acceptable and broadly-based marketing strategy is the acknowledgement that marketing activities have always been undertaken even if they have not been recognized as such. In the past the marketing aspects of many of the educational activities were not overtly identified. The purpose of the garden fête held by a primary school was seen to be fund-raising rather than image-building. The primary school holding a parents' evening to discuss how parents can be involved in classroom activities was concerned about parental support rather than parental choice. Even activities which were more apparently promotional were still viewed in educational rather than marketing terms. The secondary school's Christmas pantomime was presented as representative of the school's drama curriculum and not a publicity exercise. The reception for potential employers by the further education college to launch a newly developed course was clearly a marketing exercise but tended to be regarded solely in terms of establishing school–industry links as a wholly educational exercise. The reluctance to view these as marketing activities was because a narrow view of marketing prevailed which regarded it as a form of competition with other schools.

Yet such activities clearly fit Kotler and Fox's view that marketing involves programmes aimed at target markets to achieve institutional objectives. During the period from the 1960s into the 1980s each school had considerable freedom to evolve its own ideology and develop its own practice. Many schools developed strong links with parents, the local community, industry, and other groups with an interest in education. It was admittedly a slow, piecemeal development rather than a wholesale movement and in many cases the links formed with the various outside bodies were largely on the school's terms. Education, like other public sectors, has tended to regard the recipients of what they provide as beneficiaries rather than clients; but, nevertheless, there has been a discernible general trend towards greater openness and increased responsiveness to the multiple interested parties in education. It can be argued that this trend arose from a deepening commitment to professional accountability rather than to market accountability but in practice the result is a recognition of the need to be more responsive to consumers. This acceptance makes it possible to suggest that a consumer orientation can be a key element in developing an overall strategy for the school and to use marketing concepts as tools for planning such a strategy. Certainly the world of marketing can suggest useful questions which we in education should consider and, in seeking answers to these questions, we may reassess our assumptions and perhaps examine some of the values which underpin our practice.

Who are our customers?

Ultimately every organization, including a school, exists to satisfy the needs and wants of its clients. Identifying markets and determining customer needs/wants is an essential initial task if schools are to develop and design an organizational strategy based on client satisfaction. This poses a difficult problem for education: just who is our customer? Is it the student? Is it the parent? Is it the potential future employer? Whose needs/wants are we to meet – the individual's, industry as a whole, the country's economic needs, the needs of society, the requirements of governmental policy? There is little point in recognizing the centrality of the consumers unless it is possible to identify who they are. One attempt to categorize the marketplace of education has been to identify a three-fold classification as follows:

- The consumer market, that is, parents and pupils.
- The employment market, that is, industry, commerce and the public sector.
- The government market, that is, central and local government bodies.

This classification helps to extend the commonly held interpretation of the term *customer* and leads to the broader concept of *stakeholder*. The stakeholder concept holds that the actions of an organization should take into consideration all its publics, a public being defined as a 'distinct group of people and/or organizations that have an actual or a potential interest and/or impact on an organization' (Kotler 1975). It is suggested that a marketing philosophy implies that a school should recognize its dependence upon multiple publics for support and that it is thus necessary to develop constructive relationships with its stakeholders. There remains the central difficulty of reconciling the differing demands; attempting to be all things to all people has to be avoided. Like other public sector organizations, schools pursue multiple, non-financial, qualitative objectives, but these should not be determined by the school alone by claiming professional justification. Rather it suggests that the first step is to explore the needs/wants of its stakeholders, to establish priorities among these, and to determine objectives based on these priorities. The specific questions to be asked by the school are:

- How clearly have we identified our stakeholders?
- In what ways can the various stakeholders influence or make demands on us?
- How thoroughly are the needs/wants of our stakeholders identified?
- How can the needs/wants of the various stakeholders be reconciled?
- What priorities do we establish in relation to these?
- How effectively do we manage key stakeholders?

What is the nature of the external environment?

A marketing perspective stresses the need to examine the environment within which the school operates so that the need for crisis management arising from unanticipated circumstances can be avoided. Organizations that are able to foresee developments in the external environment which will make an impact on them are better able to respond creatively and to adapt more successfully to changed conditions. As indicated in Chapter 1 schools are operating in an increasingly turbulent environment and are facing unfamiliar challenges. It is essential that a detailed analysis is made of the reality of the threats and opportunities the Education Reform Act presents.

A well established technique in marketing which explores the capacity of an organization to meet its external challenges is to engage in a SWOT analysis, that is, an honest and detailed examination of the organization's strengths and weaknesses, opportunities and threats. Strengths identified could range from a 'reputation as a caring community' to 'situated on a main bus route'; weaknesses from 'an imbalanced staffing structure' to 'an unattractive school building'; threats from 'an unsupportive local authority' to 'local social unrest'; opportunities from 'the appointment of a new headteacher' to 'the provision of new housing in the area'.

It is obviously good sense for a school to build on its strengths and to grasp its opportunities. Threats and weaknesses are less easy to deal with. Perhaps a single example may be illustrative. A school identified unruly behaviour on the buses by a tiny minority of pupils as a threat to its reputation as a well disciplined school providing a good education. Eventually the bus serving a housing estate about half a mile from the school was withdrawn by the bus company. Possible responses by the school were:

- to regard behaviour on buses as outside the school's control;
- to rely on increased good publicity to counteract the threat;
- to tackle the threat with positive direct action.

The school took the last course and negotiated with the bus company for the service to be reinstated as a special school bus and insisted that the school should have more direct control over behaviour on the bus. Pupils were issued by the school with passes, with photograph attached, and it was announced that these could be withdrawn at the discretion of the school. The legality has never been challenged as it has not been necessary to withdraw any passes. It was a successful marketing strategy to maintain the school's positive image.

Since marketing is a force which should pervade the entire school it must enter the thinking and behaviour of all decision-makers regardless of their level in the school and their functional area. The assessment of the school's strengths, weaknesses, opportunities, and threats requires a collegial approach. The headteacher and the board of governors are not the sole arbiters. A SWOT analysis could profitably be on the agenda for a full Baker Day, carefully planned to allow various groupings to contribute their perceptions of the realities of the situation. If we fully accept the stakeholder concept it is reasonable to suggest that it is not only teachers who should be involved in the exercise but ways should be explored to include *significant others*: governors, parents, ancillary staff, LEA advisers, for example. It may be that pupils are the best judges of a school's strengths and weaknesses. The important thing is to engage in an open examination of the issues and to formulate a comprehensive and co-ordinated response based on the findings.

The broad questions to be asked are:

- How proactive rather than reactive are we to the external environment?
- How well do we read developments and trends in the environment?
- How responsive are we to events 'out there'?
- What procedures have we for assessing strengths, weaknesses, opportunities, threats?
- How successfully do we develop strategies for managing our external environment?

What business are we in?

This is a crucial question but it is not a new one. It would be possible to point to an illustrious line of great thinkers who have addressed the issue in terms of the aims of education. But the question 'What business are we in?' has a slightly different emphasis from the question 'What are the aims of education?' It has a more practical ring about it, and seems to recognize more explicitly the presence of the consumer. For too long the assumption appeared to be that the determination of the purposes and practices of education was the prerogative of the professionals alone. It is for this reason that the term *business* is used here though other terms might be more acceptable in education. The school's *mission*, for example, sounds more noble and on management courses it is not unusual to invite participants to write mission statements for the school. In the end the expressions used, whether business, mission, purposes, aims and objectives, reason for being or whatever, are not of particular importance. What is stressed here is that the answers sought can be determined within the context of an assessment of stakeholders' needs/wants set against an analysis of the schools' external environment and internal capacities. This reverses the usual approach in education, in which the schools' aim and objectives are established as a starting point.

It is not, however, a matter of finding what the stakeholders want and providing it. This, in any case, would not be possible given the many and often conflicting viewpoints. Individual teachers will have a set of basic values relating to deeply held beliefs and these will tend to be reflected in the culture and aspirations of the school. This set of values provides the bottom line for the school's mission statement but specific objectives and attainable targets can be set up by a clear understanding and acceptance of the market. Not that it is easy. Schools have multiple objectives and establishing an order of priority may not be easy. It is also likely that there are conflicting objectives among individuals and groupings within the school as well as among the stakeholders. Reference to market realities should help rather than hinder the mediation of these conflicts.

- How effectively does our strategic plan integrate stakeholder needs and our main concerns?
- Have we procedures for checking the fit between what we are achieving and what the market desires?
- To what extent do we attempt to influence the external environment and modify demands made on us?

What is our public image?

It is only when the issues identified above have been addressed that the school can deal constructively with the remaining aspect of marketing, namely, promotion. Greenall (1988), an independent public-relations consultant, offers a brief but incisive statement of some of the main issues relating to how schools can set about projecting a positive image.

He suggests that schools which have been taking public-relations seriously will reap the harvest of time and effort invested because public relations policies are more effective in achieving long-term benefits than in solving short-term problems and crises. He makes the point forcibly that it is not about the kind of competition at the periphery referred to earlier in this chapter:

> I'm not talking about window dressing. A shop that has attractive steel-front windows but offers shoddy goods, indifferent service and poor value for money is indulging in propaganda, not public relations. Nor does public relations activity consist only in obtaining favourable press coverage - another popular misconception.
>
> (TES 15 January 1988:25)

A survey of local newspapers reveals that there has been a sudden spate of news items and photographs relating to school activities many of which fail to represent the day-to-day reality of school life. There does appear to be an excessive reliance on trying to trump the efforts of rivals in selling themselves to the community.

Promotion involves everyone

The point needs to be reinforced that promotion is an important element in an overall and cohesive marketing strategy. The literature on marketing in business refers to the marketing mix as the four Ps: product, price, promotion, and place. Clearly the usefulness of the concept of the marketing mix is limited in its application to the marketing of the intangible services like education, but the task of getting the product right and promoting it effectively is of crucial importance. It was argued earlier that marketing is a force which should pervade the entire school and the same argument holds for public relations.

Given the greater openness of schools more teachers are directly involved now in public relations whether or not they recognize it as such. There are few, if any, schools where all teachers do not at various times have direct contact with parents. The messages transmitted in these contacts project a reality which is more influential than many of the overt advertising activities. Is the school atmosphere cheerful and welcoming? Are offices and interview areas comfortable? Are parents made to feel important? Are waiting times kept to a minimum? Are parents encouraged to provide honest and open feedback? In the past, contact between schools and local industry and commerce may have been mainly by senior and careers staff but, with the development of comprehensive work-experience programmes in secondary schools, almost all teachers are now involved in placement visits before, during and after the programme. Teachers and pupils are ambassadors of the school on these occasions and carry the school's reputation to a wider public. Are appointments made at the convenience of the firm or of the school? Are appointments kept on time? Is the school businesslike in its approach? Are arrangements carefully planned in full detail? Are the marketing potentialities of the programme recognized and developed? Is feedback sought on the performance of the school in organizing the programme rather than just on pupil performances? The extension of school visits in both curricular and non-curricular areas in primary and secondary schools alike inevitably presents images to an external audience. Are such visits clearly recognized as having important public relations aspects?

Promotion needs managing

It was argued earlier that the headteacher should not become a public-relations or advertising expert at the expense of the overriding responsibility for providing academic leadership within the school. Yet there are two important managerial roles involved. The headteacher's managerial responsibility for marketing a positive image of the school starts inevitably with self-presentation. As the main representative, spokesperson and liaison link with the various publics the headteacher's personality and style is important. There is, of course, a wider responsibility beyond personal impression management. In creating a market consciousness throughout the school the lead must come from the top. Marketing is a pervasive attitude and a continuous process rather than a one-off response to crisis. This attitude will not develop by chance and requires a proactive top management strategy.

The effective management of public relations is also likely to require the appointment of a teacher at senior level with specific responsibility for organizing and administering PR initiatives. This has been a common response in many schools and has much to commend it provided that the appointment is seen as a means of supporting the efforts of all teachers rather than relieving them of their responsibility for improving the school's image. Obviously it makes sense to ensure that the person appointed has enthusiasm and aptitude for the task, has ability to establish positive links with outside agencies, good written and oral communication skills, and the capacity to win the support of colleagues and key non-teaching staff who are often the first contact with the public.

A final point needs to be made about the management of marketing. Although a logical and systematic management strategy is suggested, the problems of implementing it in the political reality of school life is recognized. It cannot be introduced as a final plan providing a kind of

Monday morning solution. Successful implementation will require the exercise of sensitive political skills which recognize the existence of conflicting interests and perceptions. A particular problem may be that perceived values underpinning a market orientation may be alien to the culture of the school. Schools, like other social organizations develop unique norms, values and beliefs which result in established, accepted patterns of behaviour which are difficult to change. This chapter has suggested a series of questions which need to be addressed rather than presented recipes for success. The task will not be easy but it may, in the language of the market, prove profitable.

References

Greenall, J. (1988) 'How to improve your image', *Times Educational Supplement*, 15 January 1988: 25.

Kotler, P., (1975) *Marketing for Non-Profit Organizations*, Hemel Hempstead: Prentice Hall.

Kotler, P. and Fox, K.A. (1985) *Strategic Marketing for Educational Institutions*, Hemel Hempstead: Prentice Hall.

Russell, W. (1988) *Promoting a Positive Image*, London: The Industrial Society.

Chapter six

The legal context

Gareth Parry

The Education Reform Act 1988 amends the law relating to education. Since the Act amends rather than replaces existing law it follows that schools operate in a legal context which still rests on the foundation of earlier acts, particularly the 1944 Act. Nevertheless, the 1988 Act promulgates major new policies and sets out in great detail rules, procedures, and extensive reporting requirements.

One of the fundamental reforms of the Act is the expansion and development of financial and local management of schools. The purpose of this chapter is to examine the legal implications of financial delegation and local management as they affect schools and to comment on the mechanisms and controls that will be used to try to accomplish these radical reforms. It will try to foresee possible legal difficulties that will confront the operation of local management schemes and will attempt to assess the effect of such detailed regulations and reporting requirements on governors and heads. The problem is that law is developed through precedent and few cases arising directly from the new legislation have come before the courts. In these circumstances it is appropriate to try to anticipate possible legal difficulties by looking at relevant experience in the USA.

The Act extends the concept of financial delegation which was introduced in the Education Act (No.2) 1986. The curricular duties of the Education Act 1944 and Education Act (No.2) 1986 have been extended under the Act by the introduction of the National Curriculum and its attendant requirements. The Act also greatly increases the responsibilities of governing bodies and so supersedes some of the previous legislation.

Extensive financial and managerial duties are delegated to governing bodies under the Act. According to DES Circular 7/88 the underlying principle of local management is to secure the maximum delegation of financial and managerial responsibilities to governing bodies that is consistent with the discharge by the Secretary of State and by the LEA of their continuing statutory responsibilities. The stated objectives of local management schemes are to enable governing bodies to manage their resources effectively, including staffing, and to allow governors and headteachers to be more accountable to their clients – parents, pupils, the local community, and employers – and more responsive to their needs.

The legislative framework for local management is set out in sections 33–51, and Schedule 3 of the Act. The detailed practical considerations are set out in DES Circular 7/88 *Education Reform Act: Local Management of Schools*. Chapter 3 examines in detail issues arising from the devolution to school level of financial management. However, in order to consider the legal dimensions involved it is useful to provide a brief summary of the new financial regulations.

Under the Act each LEA (apart from the ILEA) is required to submit a local management scheme to the Secretary of State for approval. The schemes must be prepared in consultation with the governing body and headteachers of all the schools covered by the scheme. Schemes of local management will consist of two elements or processes – formula funding and delegation of budgets.

All the primary (excluding nursery and special) and secondary schools maintained by a LEA will be given a budget worked out on the basis of a resource allocation formula devised by the LEA. The schemes will come into force on 1 April 1990. The amount allocated to each of the schools is known as its budget share and schools cannot be funded more or less generously than their budget shares, except in the case of specific contingencies, for example, major emergencies which cause serious damage to schools.

The management of the budget share of each primary or secondary school with 200 or more pupils must be delegated to the governing body of that school. Responsibility for delegated budgets will be phased in between April 1990 and April 1993 (April 1992 to April 1994 for the LEAs of the former ILEA). The LEA has discretion to extend delegation to smaller primary schools (and also to special schools but not to nursery schools), but, even if a school is not in receipt of a delegated budget, expenditure must be contained within the budget share as determined by the resource-allocation formula.

The Secretary of State has the power to approve or reject the local management schemes, or approve them with modifications, or in certain circumstances, either where the LEA fails to submit a scheme or submits a scheme which does not meet with approval, the Secretary of State will have the powers to impose his own scheme.

The introduction of local management schemes will alter the role of LEAs. They will not be able to exercise detailed control over the bulk of spending in schools with delegated budgets. Their role will become more strategic and they will have important responsibilities for monitoring and evaluating the schemes. LEAs will be responsible for the following functions:

- determining the total resources available to schools;
- deciding the scope of delegation within the framework of the Act;
- establishing the basis for allocating resources to individual schools;
- setting out the conditions and requirements under which governing bodies must operate;
- monitoring the performance of schools and giving advice, or taking corrective action if necessary;
- operating sanctions, including withdrawal of delegation, where appropriate;
- providing guidance to governing bodies and heads on legal, personnel, and financial matters;
- providing for the professional development of teachers, including appraisal and in-service education;
- providing advice and support for governors of voluntary schools.

Some of the general issues and possible legal difficulties and challenges which arise out of local management schemes may be identified. The legalization of education whereby the introduction and implementation of major reforms is subject to elaborate rules, procedures, reporting requirements, and sanctions is a recent phenomenon in Britain and is graphically illustrated by the Act and its subsequent Circulars. The overall objectives of the Act are laudable – to improve standards of teaching and learning in schools. To this end the rules and regulations are designed to promote impartial decision-making, accountability, administrative consistency and efficiency, reduce uncertainty and arbitrariness, introduce flexibility, choice and competition, and reduce centralized bureaucracy. But the extent, complexity and technicality of the rules and procedures, though rational in themselves, together with the brisk timetable for reform, will give rise to difficulties in interpretation and compliance, particularly given the large number of governing bodies involved and the fact that local management is being introduced simultaneously throughout England and Wales, without the benefit of a full pilot scheme beforehand. In cases of difficulty concerning interpretation and compliance, it may be a matter for the courts to resolve. LEAs and governing bodies may fail to observe all the demands and requirements of DES Circular 7/88. Indeed some, for a variety of reasons, may not be capable of implementing all the changes regardless of the law.

Already there are indications that proper consultation between LEAs and governing bodies regarding the draft consultative schemes is not taking place and is being treated by some LEAs as 'something of a formality' (Pearce 1989). This is because of the enormous amount of time and effort that would be required to do the consultation properly and the pressure LEAs are under to finalize their plans for submission to the Secretary of State by the set date. This situation, which is not in compliance with the law, is unfortunate, since if the financial schemes are to work they will have to gain the support and acceptance of the governing bodies whose task it is to implement them. There should be no objection to consultation between LEA and governing bodies on the budget formula since nobody wants a local collective dispute involving individual schools. The active involvement of governing bodies in consultation with LEAs over local management schemes would help to reconcile the local voluntary efforts of governors with central policy initiatives which are an important feature of the Act.

The LEA officers, whose task it is to produce the financial formulae and budgets according to the government's guidelines, may produce comprehensive uniform schemes that deal in averages (aggregates) rather than with the position, rights and well-being of individual children or groups of children, or individual schools. It is certain that tensions and challenges will develop from this approach as schools discover whether they are 'winners' or 'losers'. It is probable that groups will campaign against formula funding if they feel that their children, schools, or union members are being disadvantaged by the formulae. Already, the general secretary of the National Association of Head Teachers has reportedly 'written to all CEOs in England and Wales suggesting that they should challenge the Government's funding formula in the courts'. (*Education* 19 May 1989).

Clearly, under local management, formula funding and delegated budgets become the bases of the finance of schools. As such, the formula or budget becomes the instrument of control as well as of planning. The aim of operating schools on this basis is to manage the resources effectively, to promote prudent fiscal policies, to redistribute resources, to enhance public accountability and to provide information on educational costs and priorities. The implications of this arrangement will be profound. While operating a delegated budget will force governing bodies to examine in detail all the priorities and activities of the school, no amount of careful planning will make up for inadequate funds. An example was recently highlighted in the *Times Educational Supplement* (28 April 1989) where the King's School, Peterborough, a maintained school, is experiencing financial difficulties brought about by a budgetary inadequacy. These problems prompted the head to write to the parents telling them that 'the amount of money coming through this school is not enough to continue with the present provision of staffing, books and equipment, let alone to look towards improving the standard of education King's can offer'. Obviously, fiscal reductions may have substantial effects on the working conditions of schools.

If experience in the United States of America is of any validity, then, given the similarities of the two legal systems, we can expect legal challenge to be made to the resource-allocation formulae. There, 'the uses of multiple variable factors including that of "need" in distribution formulae has gained increasing judicial, as well as political acceptance' (Valente 1987:484). School finance formulae exist in the USA which take into account cost and need differentials to a much greater extent than the age-weighted formulae in England and Wales. In addition, they include such factors as extra funding for teachers with advanced qualifications and years of experience. If such factors were incorporated into our formulae they would go some way to reassuring teachers of the fairness of formula funding. Unless flexibility can be introduced into the components that make up the formulae it is probable that we will see litigation which focuses on the propriety of age-weighted formulae.

The American acceptance of multiple variable factors has been gained over a period of about twenty years during which time school finance litigation has shown itself to be a major battlefield. The plaintiffs have attempted to establish minimum entitlement provisions. There have been a variety of legal strategies adopted, many of them under the broad banner of equal education opportunity. This is itself a problematical concept because it encompasses so many different definitions 'and one man's equal education opportunity may well be another man's law suit' (Levin 1975:411). One major approach focused on equal access to school resources, be they money, facilities, or services. In discussing fiscal inequities the difference in per-pupil expenditures among the states has long been such a topic of discussion and disagreement, as it threatens to become under local management schemes. Many of the state courts attempted to bring about more equitable school financing systems, but the path to reform was not easy and serious setbacks were experienced.

A creative legal approach was to focus on the relationship of the level of per-pupil expenditures to the quality of education – the cost–quality issue. One of the most thorough examinations of these issues was carried out in the school finance case of *Serrano v Priest* 1971, where the trial judge believed that there was a relationship between money spent per pupil and the quality of educational opportunity. The trial judge concluded that 'a school district's per pupil expenditure does play a significant role in determining whether pupils are receiving a low-quality or a high-quality program as measured by pupil test score results on the standardized achievement tests' (Levin 1975:433). However, the United States Supreme Court found that it was not possible to show a relationship between spending and educational opportunity.

One major problem with legal decisions which have been made by judges concerning education is that they are often too abstract to be of great value to school authorities. For example, in the Serrano case the California Supreme Court declared that the quality of a pupil's public education is not permitted to be 'a function of the wealth of . . . [a pupil's] parents and neighbours'. This negative standard or principle came to be known as 'fiscal neutrality'. But in practice it was difficult for school authorities to put it into practice since they were unsure whether pupils or taxpayers were the beneficiaries of the principle. What the new principle did, however, was to promote a rash of legal actions across America as 'reform-minded lawyers eagerly seized upon this standard and headed for the nearest court-house' (Levin 1975:430). One of the benefits of the years of litigation into the financing of schools has been to encourage, in the words of one judge, a movement towards less 'chaotic and unjust systems'. The extent to which courts in England and Wales will be prepared to examine such matters remains to be seen.

An important feature of the 1988 Act is that the LEA is empowered as an ultimate sanction to suspend a governing body's right to a delegated budget where it appears that the governing body:

(a) has been guilty of a substantial or persistent failure to comply with any requirement under the scheme; or
(b) it is not managing the appropriation or expenditure of the sum at its disposal for the purposes of the school in a satisfactory manner.

Though this appears a straightforward procedure and the governing body does have the right of appeal to the Secretary of State, in practice it may be rather a difficult issue and may lead to legal dispute. For example, the governing body may dispute the facts of the case: they may believe that there has been unfairness on the part of the LEA; they may question whether the procedures and policies regarding local management have always been consistently interpreted and applied by the LEA; they may claim that the advice, support, and documentation of the LEA have not been satisfactorily provided. Possibly, it may be the task of a court to resolve such a dispute, and even to overturn the decisions of the LEA if there appears to be abuse or failure on their part.

The issue of compliance with rules and regulations is a very important issue and lies at the heart of the legislation, but it is also a very difficult and sensitive matter. One of the major problems of the Act is that the rules and regulations are too detailed and rigid, and allow for little discretion on the part of governing bodies. It has been argued by Berman (1986) that the theory of compliance is far too simple for complex social systems such as the education service. Berman examined the theoretical assumptions that underlay the theory and found them to be faulty. The assumption was that schools can comply with the law or regulations. However, in reality, though schools may be willing to comply, they may not have the capacity to do so. Schools vary greatly in their local circumstances and some will be able to adapt to the new powers and responsibilities much more quickly than others. Second, compliance is not necessarily a discrete, definable act or event bounded in time and substance. Rather it is a process which takes time to develop. Certainly, it will require more time than the present timetable permits for many governing bodies and headteachers to adjust psychologically and in other ways to the new autonomy. Lastly, the theory of compliance holds that legislation, regulation, and adjudication should establish uniform standards that should be uniformly enforced in all affected organizations. It argues that without uniform standards, there is no equity.

Berman questions this assumption since he believes that because of the great variability found among schools, compliance with the law needs to be flexibly interpreted, and one should balance the need for sanctions with incentives according to local circumstances. The Coopers and Lybrand study for the DES would seem to agree on this point, since in discussing what sanctions an LEA can exercise against a reluctant school in a local management scheme it stated that initially 'we think the only option in these (hopefully rare) circumstances would be to provide additional support, advice and encouragement' (Coopers and Lybrand 1988:33).

A possible danger is that some schools in complying with the new requirements may divert resources to deal with the letter of the law, and be deflected from the educational priorities and the needs of the children: the spirit of the legislation. Furthermore, it may well be the case that LEAs will not have the financial or technical resources to ensure full compliance on the part of the school with the proper procedures concerning local management. But what happens if a governing body misuses its delegated budget and is involved in a scandal involving waste and malpractice? Will the LEA face legal action for not discharging its statutory powers effectively?

Presumably much will depend on the financial sums involved and the disruption caused to the school, and whether there was major fault or negligence on the part of the LEA. Certainly, if legal action follows and judicial decisions are made, precedents will be set and then LEAs may have to adhere strictly to monitoring duties, irrespective of the difficulties or the educational value of the duty. Conceivably a situation could arise in which non-compliance or breach of the rules is followed by even more precise and detailed rules, and schools become enmeshed in paperwork and narrowly interpreting the legal requirements.

A fundamental issue is the principle of the delegation of authority.

The manner and scope of delegation is controlled by law, so that the responsibilities are subject to legal standards of proper and improper delegation of authority. While the principle of delegation appears straightforward, it may well prove to be extremely complicated, since it is not possible to specify all possible delegated duties. Delegated powers may not be used in bad faith, or in an unreasonable or arbitrary manner. It is quite likely that occasions will arise when there is abuse of power and it will be for the courts to determine disputed powers. It is possible that the relationship between some governing bodies and headteachers will prove to be problematic as regards their respective limits of authority under the law.

Liability of governors

It is worth re-emphasizing that the 1988 Act amends existing legislation and the legal requirements in relation to such areas as health and safety at work, care and custody of pupils and punishment remain unchanged. Nevertheless, under the new legislation, governing bodies will be more directly liable to legal proceedings. Formerly, legal cases were accepted and handled by the legal section of the LEA. In most cases, even where individual headteachers or teachers were named, the judgements were almost always made in terms of the LEA and costs and awards were covered by the authority's insurance indemnity. Recent years have seen a spate of litigation through the courts, particularly where existing law is inadequate to deal with current trends or has emerged in piecemeal fashion. Law in relation to education has been one such area and the new legislation will provide additional areas of uncertainty and complexity over legal issues. However, the public, generally, are much more aware of their legal rights and more prepared to seek redress through the courts.

Legal writers and researchers have produced a number of texts which deal in a practical way with the legal context of schools, for example, *The School Governors' Legal Guide* (Lowe 1988). Headteachers and governors are well advised to consult existing literature and keep up-to-date with legal issues as they emerge. The National Association of Head Teachers has produced an invaluable legal guide for schools, in ring binder form and updated regularly. The Association also provides its members with updated information and advice on legal matters through its journals. For example, the legal position of teachers taking children abroad is presently of concern in many schools. The NAHT Bulletin (May 1989) lists a number of useful recommendations made by the Altwood School Enquiry Panel on a ski trip which led to pupil deaths. They include the importance of governors and teachers working together to ensure satisfactory arrangements, comprehensive briefing of staff and fully informing parents in sufficient time for them to change their minds if desired.

Arising from the increased duties of governing bodies comes the thorny issue of increased liabilities. The Act makes it clear that governors will not incur any personal financial liability in respect of any contract they enter in good faith in the exercise of their delegated powers under a local management scheme. However, much depends on the interpretation of 'good faith' and it will be for the courts to review the facts on a case-by-case basis. It is possible that legal action could be taken against governing bodies for a wide range of liabilities, including malpractice, personal accidents, violating LEA regulations, or perhaps for not acting at all.

Given the extent of involvement in such sensitive areas as appointing and dismissing staff, against a background of complex and wide-ranging legislation, it is likely that the extent of governors' liabilities will be tested in the courts. Hereford and Worcester Education Committee has already asked major insurance companies to submit quotations for insuring governing bodies against liabilities not covered in the Act. As its secretary and solicitor commented, 'if the quotations are gigantic then obviously the risk is huge' (*Education*, 13 January 1989). The National Association of Governors and Managers (NAGM) advises governors to consider personal liability insurance and the National Confederation of Parent–Teacher Associations has produced a professional indemnity and liability insurance scheme. Some experts, bearing in mind school accidents such as the Austrian mountains tragedy, believe that governing bodies ought to take out personal accident insurance for the entire school.

Liabilities may arise in a wide range of areas of school life, for example, data protection, defamation and slander, discipline and control, copyright, pupil and staff records. Already, the question of access to the names and addresses in school admission registers has surfaced as a possible legal issue. Under the legislation the register must be available for parents to consult in relation to ballots for opting out, but what happens when an individual governor uses such lists for personal motives, for example, financial gain? It is possible that such a situation is a breach of confidentiality, with possible legal consequences.

Health and safety

Though local management brings no significant changes in the area of health and safety, since the LEA retains the primary responsibilities, governing bodies will have liabilities relating to the building and other school property. It may be the case that the LEA will not be held liable for damages where the injuries arise out of the negligence of the governing body, for example, failure to repair faulty equipment. Where a governing body fails to comply with the LEA's policy on health and safety, the authority should arrange for the work to be carried out and the school to be charged for the work.

Staffing

The responsibilities governing bodies will have in respect of staffing are an important and integral part of local management. Schools with delegated budgets will be able to decide on the basis of the financial resources available, how many teaching and non-teaching staff should work at the school. The LEA will no longer have the power to set the staff complement, but may wish to give advice about the staffing levels it considers necessary to secure curricular duties and which are consistent with the school's budget.

When making appointments, governing bodies will be bound by legislative provisions on race and sex discrimination. Unlawful factors relating to an applicant's race, sex, or marital status must not be used in making an appointment, and failure to observe these provisions will be answerable before an industrial tribunal. If discrimination is proved it is possible that compensation may be awarded against the governing body as individuals. Legal difficulties will arise in this area if there is a lack of training and professionalism on the part of governors. The LEA is obliged to appoint staff selected by the governing body unless the person fails to satisfy the requirements relating to qualifications, health and conduct.

Discipline, grievance, and suspension

The responsibility for disciplinary and grievance procedures will rest with the governing body who will be required to establish disciplinary rules and procedures, and procedures enabling staff to seek redress of grievances relating to their employment. Such disciplinary rules and procedures must be sufficiently clear, specific, and thorough as to what conduct or behaviour is permitted and what is proscribed. The rules and regulations regarding discipline and grievances must be issued to all staff by the governing body.

Since there is no national standard regarding appropriate disciplinary procedures in the teaching profession, governing bodies are advised to approach the LEA, teacher unions, or the Advisory Conciliation and Arbitration Service for advice and guidance in drawing up disciplinary codes and grievance procedures. However, governing bodies do not have to follow that advice and may devise their own procedures.

It will be interesting to see how soon some governing bodies will address the issue of incompetence or inefficiency on the part of teachers in their disciplinary codes. Certainly in the USA school boards regularly dismiss teachers on the grounds of incompetence. Governing bodies will be able to discipline, suspend or dismiss teachers, or if that function is exercised by the LEA then they will be able to ask the LEA to comply with a request to discipline a teacher. The LEA cannot dismiss a teacher who is employed in a school with a delegated budget. At all times governing bodies must carefully follow the disciplinary rules issued to staff. On an appeal to an industrial tribunal the sanctions or penalties may be reduced if they are considered to be unreasonable.

Clearly such disciplinary measures which may affect employment rights are quasi-judicial in their operation and as such must be treated with the greatest caution since the courts will examine the legal justification for such actions.

In a salutary and much publicized American case, *Eckmann v Board of Education of Hawthorn School District*, a local school board dismissed a teacher who had become an unwed mother on the grounds of 'immorality'. However, the child was conceived as a result of a rape and the 'jury demonstrated its outrage towards the board by awarding the teacher a 3.3 million dollar verdict' (Sacken 1988:281). The decision to dismiss Eckmann was described as a 'huge and expensive managerial error' (Sacken 1988:297) on the part of the school board.

A major problem facing governing bodies in possible discipline and dismissal proceedings is that the procedures required by law are much more formal and rigorous than may be assumed by a lay critic.

Dismissal

A controversial section of the Act deals directly with dismissal. The arrangement for dismissal puts the responsibility on the governing body to decide whether or not someone employed at the school should cease to work there. It is certain that reduced enrolments, budget shortfalls, and changes in curriculum policy will require governing bodies to reduce staffing and cause the release of surplus teachers. Providing the governors act reasonably and in good faith, base their actions upon clear and reasonable evidence, take advice from the LEA and carry out the correct procedures, their decisions regarding dismissal will prevail.

The burden of showing that there has been a fault or an abuse in law will be upon the dismissed teacher, and governors will have to defend their actions personally if the dismissed teacher complains to an industrial tribunal. It is likely that teachers who face dismissal under local management will challenge on the grounds that their position was not lawfully terminated, that dismissal was in breach of contract, that the proper procedures were not carried out, or that teachers other than themselves should have been the candidates for dismissal.

The governors will not have to meet the costs of dismissal from the delegated budget unless the LEA has good reason for passing on the costs, for example, where the LEA considered that such a dismissal was unreasonable and likely to be found unfair before an industrial tribunal. A possible scenario for this might be that a teacher is dismissed and then replaced by a teacher lower on the pay scale. That would not constitute a redundancy.

In the USA, school dismissal and school employment cases are common, and among recent reported cases are instances where a school board attempted to employ a substitute teacher for a vacant full-time position. Another involved an appeal by a teacher regarding the amendment of his contract from full-time to part-time because of a reduction in the teaching complement. A very pertinent case was where a teacher appealed a dismissal on funding grounds.

> The teacher contended that the board reduced teaching positions in response to funding cuts without demonstrating a justification for decreasing the number of teaching positions. The board simply contended that its decision was not arbitrary and capricious as they followed policy regarding reduction in personnel. *Held*: For teacher. Before the board could decrease the number of teaching positions in its district, it needed to prove that the reduction in the professional staff was justified . . . The mere fact that funding had been cut was not sufficient evidence to prove that reduction in professional staff was justified.
>
> (Journal of Law and Education 1989:164-5)

Teacher appraisal

The government's national steering group on teacher appraisal may recommend that governing bodies will not have access to the appraisal records of teachers, though it appears that they may comment on headteachers' appraisal by the LEA. The legal reason for this is that LEAs remain the teachers' formal employer and that such rights, which are contained in contracts of employment, cannot be extended to governing bodies and that teacher appraisal is to be regarded as a purely professional matter. So LEAs will have unilateral control over the appraisal process under the Education Act (No.2) 1986. This recommendation if accepted could cause difficulties for governing bodies and it would be surprising if it were not legally challenged by governing bodies. The issue poses a number of legal ambiguities. One could argue that the governing body interest in appraisal records is a valid one, and denial of access complicates their management role and goes against much of the underlying philosophy of the Act.

Hinds, convenor of the appraisal sub-committee of the NAGM, recently said that 'governors must be free to contribute evidence during the initial appraisal period, not least because they had legal responsibility for personnel issues'. He added that 'governors are the only people with the power to build on the strengths and weaknesses of teachers. The way they perceive staff is both unique and relevant' (*Education* 16 June 1989).

In the *TES* (30 June 1989) a 'News' item reported that, in a position statement issued by the NAGM, it was argued that governors had to be involved in appraisal interviews and take responsibility for the judgements made. It is not difficult to envisage legal conflict in this very sensitive area, and it could well exemplify the central issue of LEA v. governing bodies control, which may be a major issue in future litigation.

Also in the case of teachers and heads who have received poor appraisal reviews what financial and managerial burdens might be placed on governing bodies in trying to bring about improvements? In other words, what will it cost to salvage a poor teacher, and who will pay the costs?

Obviously when a full appraisal scheme emerges the details of the contract concerning appraisal must specify unequivocally the stages, procedures, documentation, appeals procedure, and possibly disciplinary actions allowable by law. The American experience of appraisal shows it to be a very fertile field for litigation. There the process plays a key role in employment decisions such as tenure, contracts, demotions, suspension, and dismissal.

Charges for school activities

The Act recognizes the principle of free school education but believes that LEAs and schools should be able to resort to charges for optional activities which are provided out of school hours. DES Circular 2/89 attempted to clarify the legislative provisions on charges. The charging provisions came into effect on 1 April 1989. Among the provisions are that education provided during school hours (mid-day break is excluded) is free of charge to all pupils, with the exception of individual tuition in a musical instrument, except where it is provided to fulfil statutory requirements when it must be provided free. LEAs and schools are, however, given discretionary powers to charge for optional activities provided wholly or mainly out of school hours, as long as these activities are not required to meet the statutory duties relating to the curriculum or prescribed examinations. It is a requirement of the Act that LEAs must provide parents with a statement of policy on charging and remissions so that parents are clear from the outset what approach is being adopted. No charge can be levied unless LEAs and schools have drawn up a statement of policy and parents have been informed.

There may be occasions when a third party arranges activities to take place in schools. The third party unfortunately is not defined, and it will be a task for the courts to do so. The third party, quite likely to be a tour operator, would be able to levy charges directly on the parents for the services provided. Then the Circular states that:

> The LEA and school governing body would not take part in the transaction and it would be for parents, and any staff members similarly released for the activity, to satisfy themselves about the adequacy of the arrangements made by the third party to secure the safety and welfare of the children.

(DES Circular 2.89)

This statement is confusing in the extreme since it blurs the degree of involvement and responsibility of LEAs and schools for the safety and welfare of children. The Association of County Councils has pointed out 'that if teachers wished to participate in visits arranged by a third party, they would have to negotiate their own separate contract with the third party' (*Education* 20 January 1988). There are real dangers here for individual teachers since they may be held legally responsible should anything go wrong on a trip.

Although no compulsory charges may be made, except as noted above, LEAs and governing bodies may invite parents to make voluntary contributions for the benefit of the school or any school activity. These contributions must be genuinely voluntary and, in inviting parents to contribute, it must be made clear that there is no obligation to do so and that pupils whose parents have not contributed will not be treated any differently from others. There is no limit to the level of voluntary contributions that parents can make to school activities.

There is nothing to prevent schools from asking parents to pay for the cost of replacing items like broken apparatus or lost textbooks where the damage or loss has resulted from the behaviour of their children. Governing bodies are advised to include their policy on such matters in their code of discipline so that pupils and parents know where they stand. But the DES accept that such a contract would be unlikely to be legally enforceable.

The details contained in the circular are complex and will place heavy demands on schools. The basic principles outlined are reasonably clear apart from the paragraph dealing with the activities arranged by a third party, but in their application to the circumstances in any particular school or any particular activity difficult questions of interpretation may occur. Difficulties and confusions are already being experienced in relation to school visits and trips which take place mainly during school hours. It is likely that this section of the Act will be challenged as contrary to the law which upholds the principle of 'free' education in maintained schools. It remains to be seen what interpretation judicial opinion will make of the working and what activities and services should be included in free public education.

Financial provisions and competitive tendering

It is not proposed to deal in detail with the financial responsibilities of governing bodies under the Act, other than to point out that they must observe the specific legal guidelines laid down by the LEA regarding finance and accounting procedures. Delegated budgets will be subject to auditing and accounting procedures under the supervision of the LEA. Governing bodies, though they have discretion as to how sums may be spent, must not permit spending for improper purposes, for example, donating sums to a political party. Should anyone divert funds for personal use, he or she would be held personally liable and would probably face criminal charges.

In addition, difficulties may arise over the very complex issues relating to contracts and competitive tendering. The matter is much too technical to be dealt with here, but it is the case that great care needs to be taken to ensure that fraud, collusion and favouritism are avoided. Recent changes in the Schools Government Regulations are concerned to 'exclude anyone who has spent long periods in prison and to make sure teachers and others do not profit from "undue influence" on the governing body' (Doe 1989). It would be most unusual if serious legal difficulties do not arise in financial matters relating to local management.

Conclusion

It was clear for a number of years that a major Education Act was needed to clear up many of the confusions, ambiguities and legal difficulties that emerged from the Education Act 1944, but paradoxically the degree and extent of the legalisation associated with the 1988 Act may well cause many diverse and complicated legal challenges. It is anticipated that increased rates of litigation will result from the Act. Nevertheless, the charge made by American school officials who complain that one must be a lawyer to operate a school, one hopes, will be avoided.

In part, the American misfortune regarding school litigation arose out of a movement in the first decades of this century to make education more efficient, accountable and cost-effective. The movement was based on the principles of scientific management, and cost-accounting and performance indicators were major features of management practice. As Callahan (1962) showed, a great tragedy was inflicted on the education system:

> Educational questions were subordinated to business consider-ations; administrators were produced who were not, in any true sense, educators; that a scientific label was put on some very unscientific and dubious methods and practices; and an anti-intellectual climate, already prevalent, was strengthened. As the business–industrial values and procedures spread into the thinking and acting of educators, countless educational decisions were made on economic or on non-educational grounds.
>
> (Callahan 1962: 246–7)

While it is important that schools are aware of the legal minefield that emerges from the Act, educational principles should be paramount. A decision is not a good decision simply because it avoids legal difficulties.

References

Berman, P. (1986) 'From compliance to learning: implementing legally induced reform', in *School Days, Rule Days*, D.L. Kirp and D.N. Jensen (eds) London: Falmer Press.

Callahan, R.E. (1962) *Education and the Cult of Efficiency*, Chicago: University of Chicago Press.

CIPFA (1988) *Local Management in Schools*, London: The Local Management in Schools Initiative.

Coopers and Lybrand (1988) *Local Management of Schools*, London: HMSO.

Croner Publications *The Head's Legal Guide*, New Malden.

DES (1988) *Education Reform Act: Local Management of Schools*, Circular 7/88, London: HMSO.

DES (1989) *Education Reform Act 1988: Charges for School Activities*, Circular 2/89, London: HMSO.

Doe, B. (1989) 'DES lists key tasks governors must retain', *Times Educational Supplement*, 2 June.

Levin, B. (1975) 'Recent developments in the law of equal educational opportunity', *Journal of Law and Education*, vol. 4, no. 3.

Lowe, C. (1989) *The School Governor's Legal Guide*, 2nd edn, New Malden: Croner Publications.

NAHT (1989) *Guide to the Education Reform Act, 1988*, Haywards Heath.

Pearce, J. (1989) 'Intricate sums', *Education* 19 May.

Sacken, D.M. (1988) 'Bad management makes bad law', *Journal of Law and Education*, vol. 17, no. 2.
Valente, W.D. (1987) *Law in Schools*, 2nd edn, Columbus, Ohio: Merrill Publishing Company.

Chapter seven

Staff management and the school principal

Richard Mapstone

The Education Reform Act of 1988 has delegated to headteachers and governors clear responsibility for tasks such as recruitment, deployment, discipline, redundancy and dismissal. The past two decades have seen increased teacher militancy supported by teacher unions and an escalating series of disputes which in many cases has placed headteachers in an uncertain position over where their allegiance lay. In addition, the task of managing staff has been made more complex by emerging legislation relating to matters such as fair employment, equal opportunity, discriminatory practice, sexual harassment, unlawful dismissal, and grievance procedures.

Throughout the 1960s the government instituted a range of expansionist and egalitarian policies in education. It was also a period of growing penetration by central government into the arena of public-sector wages and salaries. This attempt by government to control teacher salaries was in part responsible for growing inter-union tensions, coupled with a changing age structure of the teacher population and the developing militancy and radicalism within parts of the teaching profession. The recent decade has therefore been one of increasing difficulty for teachers. Teachers continue nationally to be faced with declining roles, deteriorating working conditions, and school closures and contraction.

It has also been a period when education has been subject to intense and often adverse criticism. It is not surprising that the commonly held view is that teachers are suffering from low morale, diminished self-esteem, and increasing stress. All this is coupled with increasing centralization of decisions on the financing of education and a progressive reduction in the amount of finance available. The combination of these circumstances suggests that the management of staff needs to be handled with sensitivity and awareness of the legal and political context.

Previous chapters have explored the impact of legislation upon the various roles required of the headteacher. The new education act will not simply affect the way the headteachers fulfil their role, but will have a dramatic impact on the relationship between teachers and their headteacher, and between the headteacher, governing bodies, and local authorities. The new legislation delegates to school governors powers of hiring and firing, promoting and deploying staff, and most of the activities normally associated with those of a large employer. These key functions are therefore central to the management development of headteachers who will need to advise school governors on what is prudent and cost-effective while at the same time protecting the interests of their staff.

Traditionally, relatively little attention has been given to assisting headteachers in the complex task of staff management. A high degree of professional autonomy has characterized the staff management role of the headteacher. However, schools jeopardize their effectiveness as teaching organizations if insufficient attention is given to staff needs. Changes brought about by new legislation in education parallel similar changes in the health services and the universities and result in a much more direct staff management role for headteachers. The management of people is not separate from the other managerial functions carried out by the headteacher. The school will have a philosophy in the development of which the headteacher will have played a major part, and will have established overall policies, practices, and procedures. There are, however, a number of specific personnel activities carried out in all organizations which require particular skills, techniques, and processes. Within the framework laid down by statute it will have policies to deal with issues such as staff sickness or absence; these policies set out the steps to be followed by the school management when confronted by such problems. There are therefore within the school a range of procedures which tell the headteacher how specific issues should be handled. The new legislation, however, places additional burdens upon headteachers which may require them to create procedures where none existed before or to adapt existing procedures to make them more responsive to changing circumstances. This chapter seeks to provide some guidance for the headteacher, by looking at the manpower needs of the organization and the procedures associated with the life cycle of recruiting and developing staff.

Selection and the organization

A major aim of the headteacher and governors should be to ensure compatibility between the people recruited and the school's expectations of its hiring needs. These will be determined by curriculum needs which will be influenced significantly by the requirements of the National Curriculum. The headteacher, in advising the governors, needs

99

to be able to forecast what kinds of ability are required and in what proportions. It is only on the basis of such knowledge that the school's recruitment requirements can be accurately predicted. Through a properly developed manpower plan the school's staff recruitment can go beyond immediate requirements and anticipate and plan for requirements in the future. The key essential of a good selection process is to select the most appropriate teacher or staff member to carry out a particular set of tasks. The starting point therefore is an analysis of the job, that is, the sorting out of the elements of the job into priorities. The end result is some form of job description which outlines the key tasks and content of the job. The procedure is:

Vacancy   Job analysis
Prepare job description (that is, tasks to be done)
Prepare job specification (that is, ideal candidate qualities to do the job)
Establish appointment criteria
Advertise, combining job description and job specification
Application form: job description usually sent with form
Interview
Appoint (appointed candidate given job description)

Recruitment and selection on the basis of a job description is a process which includes both an examination of the vacancy and a study of the various sources of potentially suitable candidates. Under LMS the school can determine staffing levels within given constraints and the vacancy may have occurred as a result of the development of a new course or initiative. In all probability, therefore, the need for the new employee has been established and the school has a clear idea of what is required for the job. Most recruitment, however, will still result from transfers, promotions, and retirement. It may be possible to fill the post from within the school or by the use of part-time or temporary teachers. The use of part-time or temporary contracts is sometimes the only option available to the headteacher when the school is faced with falling rolls. However, it can create problems of low morale and poor motivation. Filling the post from within the existing resources of the school often makes better use of abilities and may be more reliable than external recruitment, since the person recruited to the vacancy will be already known to other staff and to the headteacher.

The inevitable final result, however, is often a vacancy elsewhere that has to be filled from outside. The school may therefore be faced with the task of advertising the post. The primary aim of advertising should be to attract a small number of well-qualified candidates by the quickest and cheapest means. The advertisement, therefore, represents the next stage in the school's selection process and the post and qualifications required should be described in such a way that candidates on the fringe will be deterred from applying and good candidates will be encouraged. The advertisement should contain therefore:

- a job title;
- a description of the school, its aims, and philosophy;
- a description of the job and experience and skills required to undertake the job;
- working conditions, salary, and benefits;
- the next steps required from the interested candidate.

It is important to recognize that, in the event of a complaint by a rejected candidate, this information will be regarded as part of the selection criteria.

Whatever method of recruitment is used, be it internal transfer or external recruitment, it is advised that the candidate should be asked to complete an application form. In some areas candidates have traditionally been asked to complete a letter of application with an accompanying CV. Good practice, however, would favour application forms which ensure that important details about the candidate are not omitted and information on the candidate is forthcoming in a standard, logical, and uniform manner. The layout of application forms varies but should contain:

- personal data;
- details of employment history;
- education and qualifications;
- medical history.

The application form, therefore, is not only the basis of selection, but is the fundamental document in the teacher's personal record and forms part of the teacher's contract of employment. The next task facing the headteacher is to compare the application form with the specification for the job, identifying the attributes and shortcomings of apparently suitable candidates. From this study emerges a list of those candidates to be interviewed.

Assuming that a suitable candidate has emerged from the selection process, the candidate must now receive a formal offer. The usual procedure is for an oral offer to be made which is confirmed later in writing. Particular care should be made in making the initial offer. The offer should include the following elements:

- The post should be named and any special conditions relating to the post should be outlined.
- The essential conditions of the post, the hours, the holidays, the specific tasks, should all be detailed in the offer.
- The salary offered must be sufficient to attract, whilst being consistent with the earnings of other teachers in the school.
- The offer may be qualified, in the sense that it is made subject to satisfactory references or medical examination.

Confirmation of the verbal offer in writing must therefore be a careful process since it not only forms a written record, it also forms the basis of the individual's contract of employment. The 1972 Contract of Employment Act requires that employees be given a statement of their conditions of service within the first thirteen weeks of employment. The statutory statement must contain:

- name of employer and employee;
- date when employment commences;
- pay, or method of calculating pay;
- interval at which pay is given;
- terms and conditions of work (the hours, the holidays, sick and pension provision);
- length of notice of termination required by the employer;
- note of employees' trade-union rights;
- procedures covering discipline, grievances etc.

What has been outlined so far are standard operational practices for recruitment and selection within organizations. The new education legislation will give governors and headteachers of schools considerably increased powers over the appointment and dismissal of staff. This places a particular responsibility on headteachers to monitor and be sensitive to the range of discriminations that can emerge in the selection process and become reinforced in the organization.

Women teachers and black teachers already face disadvantage in terms of appointment and promotion. This disadvantage may well increase where schools are no longer directly bound by the equal-opportunity practices of local education authorities. Schools which have opted out will, for example, no longer receive the advice and support of the LEA. The provision for opting out does not take into account the issues of gender and ethnic discrimination. The education reform legislation fails to address the issues of discrimination in education or the structures and traditions in the education system that perpetuate inequalities.

There is therefore a direct responsibility upon headteachers to face the issues of discrimination both at the stages of recruitment and selection and throughout the school. This will require headteachers to target, resource, and monitor in this area. Recruiting procedures may use 'targeting methods' such as encouraging certain staff to apply for promotion, or advertisements in the ethnic press. There should also be an ongoing monitoring process of the position of such groups within the organization. It may be, therefore, that school governors and headteachers need direct guidance on the equal opportunity dimensions of their new role.

The development of staff

The school is a complex organization of teachers at varying levels of seniority, ancillary staff, and pupils. It contains, therefore, a variety of often conflicting aims and aspirations. This has a direct effect upon the manner in which the headteacher approaches the complex area of staff relationships. The headteacher may, for example, see the role in traditional terms as one of directing and controlling the school to achieve a specific set of results, particular objectives, and targets. Such a view regards the role of headteacher to be interlinked with either governors or the LEA as representing the rule-making authority within the school. Here the school is seen in unitary terms, the headteacher representing authority and the school the sole focus of loyalty.

It may be more appropriate to view the school as a plural organization containing many related but separate interests and objectives which are required to co-exist. There are therefore, for staff, rival sources of leadership and attachment. The role of the headteacher in the context of these staff relationships is not simply to exercise authority but to develop realistic team work based upon mutual interdependence. Such a strategy in handling staff relationships is directly affected by factors both internal and external to the school.

Externally the elements of political consensus which were apparent in education in the 1960s disappeared in the 1970s under the impact of economic recession. The rapid expansion of the teacher force in the 1960s was followed by marked contraction and major shifts in control of educational expenditure from local to central government. Attempts to solve the problem of teachers' salaries have become bound up with efforts to clarify teachers' responsibilities and with efficiency. These external factors interlink with the attitudes to staff relationships that exist within the school, and the headteacher's strategy for handling staff relationships. The headteacher's aim should be the achievement of maximum co-operation and the minimum of staff unrest.

Headteachers have a major responsibility for the internal organization, management, and control of the school. They should direct their skills to establishing effective structures and processes which are as simple, clear, and understandable as possible. Central to this objective is the process of consultation and involvement undertaken by the headteacher with the school staff. The purpose of such involvement should be to advance the well-being of all concerned, and to assist the school to achieve its objectives. It should provide staff with the opportunity to contribute to the success of the school by involving them in decision-making and the joint examination of problems which involve everyone.

Many headteachers have been operating effective consultative procedures for years with the principal aim of consensus management. To be effective in this consultative role the headteacher requires a clear idea of the aims and priorities of the school. It is through such consultation that staff develop a sense of collective identity and purpose and are aware of the school's priorities. The process of consultation also provides the cornerstone to the successful appraisal and development of staff at all levels.

Within the school environment there are increasing pressures on teachers. The 1988 Act was introduced at a time when teachers were coping with the hurried introduction of a new examination system, the development of innovative curriculum programmes, changed conditions of service including directed time, and increased accountability to stakeholders. The Act imposes a national curriculum, open competition among schools, testing of pupils, and more direct accountability. Provision for schools and individual teachers to be *held to account* by governors and parents may be seen by many teachers as threatening. Inevitably there may be a tendency among some teachers to develop an 'employee versus management' attitude. This means that, however successful the consultative machinery may be within the school, there will be an inevitable increase in grievances and a consequent increase in pressure upon the headteacher.

Previously, teachers on appointment received a conditions-of-service document which referred the teacher to the procedure to be followed if the teacher had a grievance. Most authorities operated a standard grievance procedure which emphasized both the formal and informal aspects of grievances. Under the provisions of the Education Reform Act the governors must make provision for the redress of grievances related to the employment of staff. It is likely that the procedures which emerge will follow established patterns. Many grievances will occur where difficulty has arisen between members of staff and if these can be resolved using informal procedures the headteacher may not have to be involved. Even where the teacher has a grievance about working conditions it should be discussed initially with the teacher's senior staff member or head of department. If there is a failure to resolve the matter at this stage, the headteacher should be involved.

This constitutes the informal approach. It enables the teacher to be accompanied by a friend or union representative, and requires of the headteacher a range of interpersonal skills. Clearly the most efficient way to settle grievances is to obtain the facts. It is this that may prove the most difficult task for the headteacher since facts are often intermeshed with emotion and differing perceptions of situations. The headteacher requires not simply listening skills, but the ability to be able to draw from the teacher both the agreed problem and potential solutions to it. March (1974) suggests that assessment of evidence is a necessary skill for the effective manager and this is clearly one area in which it needs to be exercised. The central thrust, therefore, of grievance management must be to settle the dispute internally, simply and speedily with the least disruption. Thus the headteacher should try to settle grievances directly with the person concerned. Only if this is unsuccessful should formal procedures be instituted.

Alongside the grievances that may be raised by staff are the problems of staff discipline that inevitably arise in any organization. Within any code or policy on discipline, the rules and procedures are aimed at the promotion of fairness. Thus teachers should be aware of the disciplinary procedures that operate in the school. They should, like the grievance procedures, form part of the conditions of service documentation received at induction and may be further included in the staff manual. The main provisions of such procedures are usually general indications of the employers' right to dismiss for good cause or misconduct. This is an area that often requires interpretation by an industrial tribunal.

Effective discipline is in reality a spin-off from positive leadership by the headteacher. Most teachers will behave reasonably throughout their employment. A procedure is necessary, therefore, only for those few staff who fail to observe established rules and standards. The general character of a disciplinary procedure is that, like any policy, it should reflect the general principles of the school. It should give positive direction, prescribing what staff are expected to do, and should establish standards. What belongs, therefore, in the written procedure is a series of disciplinary steps showing that action will proceed in an orderly sequence through informality to a series of graded penalties.

The management of discipline by the headteacher is governed by several basic principles. First, the individual should know the standards of performance that are expected; second, any failing by the individual should be clearly identified; and finally the individual member of staff should be given the opportunity to improve. The headteacher needs to be aware, not only of the disciplinary procedures operating in the workplace, but also of the limits of his or her authority in dealing with such issues, and must be prepared to search for specialist expertise either through the local authority personnel services or the local office of the Advisory Conciliation and Arbitration Service (ACAS). ACAS provides often the best source of advice and guidance available locally to a headteacher. ACAS counsel that discipline should be seen in a positive manner, not exclusively in terms of dealing with offences, but rather as a means of establishing standards of conduct for staff.

There are a number of general areas of employment within which the governors may have a fair basis for dismissal. If the employee lacks the skills, abilities or physical health to perform the job, the governors may consider this as potential grounds for fair dismissal. Similarly, there may be a range of behaviours forming part of the disciplinary code within the school that would be identified as misconduct and potentially fair grounds for dismissal. These grounds may include offences relating to drink or criminal conviction or the problem of persistent absence. There are some situations where the governors may be legally barred from continuing to employ an employee. It may, for example, be considered fair to dismiss someone employed with significant driving responsibilities who has been disqualified from driving. Where an employee's job ceases to exist it is potentially fair for the employee to be dismissed on grounds of redundancy.

In all these instances it is recommended that the headteacher seeks advice before the governors embark on the process of dismissal. It should be remembered that teachers, like other groups of employees, are protected from unfair dismissal, provided they have maintained continuous employment for at least 52 weeks and work over 16 hours per week. However, the headteacher should be aware that within education not only are full-time staff used but wide use is made of part-time and temporary staff who may, in certain circumstances, acquire rights under this legislation.

The headteacher, therefore, requires an understanding of the operation of the industrial tribunal system. This system was established in the 1960s. The tribunal hears disputes between employers and employees arising from rights given to employees in law. Tribunals, therefore, hear claims covering such issues as unfair dismissal, maternity rights, suspension on medical grounds, and unfair redundancy. The tribunal itself consists of a legally qualified chairperson and two lay representatives, one generally representing employee interests and one representing employer interests. These lay representatives bring a knowledge of the world of work into the legal discussion. The tribunals have been designed to make them as voluntary and informal as possible. The aim is to provide a speedy and cheap remedy to perceived injustice. Appeal from an industrial tribunal is to the Employment Appeal Tribunal (Court of Appeal in Northern Ireland). Applicants and respondents may present their case without solicitors or barristers. The headteacher may frequently find that he or she is required to give evidence at tribunal either for or against a plaintiff about actions or decisions taken concerning particular members of staff. It is, therefore, important for headteachers to maintain a full and accurate record of discussions held with staff members and decisions taken. Thus, in the event of cross-examination, a record made at the time is a far more secure reference point than memory.

Staff appraisal and training

The development of staff throughout their career requires not simply the staff management skills essential to induction, but an understanding of the training and development of the staff within the school. Teacher appraisal has profound implications for senior teachers. The success of any appraisal scheme is dependent upon the resources which the headteacher can obtain for training and career development. Performance appraisal is therefore one of the central staff management functions that will be required of senior staff. It concerns how well someone is doing in a particular post. There are two major objectives of appraisal. First, performance appraisal can be used to evaluate the effectiveness of the school's recruitment and selection. In education there has been considerable resistance to the imposition of a formal appraisal system through which decisions about promotions, transfers, and redundancies are made. However, there could be little objection to headteachers and governors using information gained from appraisal, even if the records of individual teachers are not made available to governors, to form judgements relating to their own effectiveness in selecting and promoting staff. It could be argued that, traditionally, selection procedures in education have lacked such monitoring. Second, there are important development objectives associated with perform-ance appraisal and these form the strong argument for support by the profession of formal appraisal in education. Appraisal has the objective of developing employee skills and motivation and providing performance feedback. Teachers, like other employees, need to know what others think of their performance. Such appraisal involves giving employees guidance and direction for future performance and improve-ment, and identifying the training and developmental needs of staff.

In one sense headteachers already undertake appraisal since all managers are constantly forming judgements of their subordinates and colleagues. They are in that sense continually making appraisals. A systematic system of appraisal should, therefore, be of direct assistance to the headteacher in deciding the future motivation and training needs of staff.

Early appraisal schemes in industry and commerce used mechanistic grading, ranking, or rating methods. In recent years there has been a reaction against formal appraisal systems because of the tendency of appraisal procedures to decay rapidly into a system of routine form-filling. This, however, is a criticism of the method rather than a criticism of appraisal *per se*. Thus, more recently, more flexible, interactive, approaches have been developed. The nature of teaching and learning clearly requires the latter approach and appraisal should be an extension and formalization of the kinds of informal judgements which have always taken place. Whatever method of appraisal is used, an essential feature is that performance should be matched against realistic, shared objectives and the demands of the job. Headteachers continuously assess the merits of their subordinates and some formal structuring of this regular assessment is appropriate. The success claimed in a number of trial schemes is encouraging.

The final and most important stage of appraisal is the interview process where the appraiser discusses the appraisal with the teacher. In the interview process the individual learns where he/she stands in the organization and is counselled about how performance may be improved. This is often the most difficult stage since it relies upon a range of interactive skills which the headteacher may or may not possess. The interview should therefore be planned to emphasize areas of good performance and those in need of improvement, to focus upon development and to invite participation. In the interview there should be opportunities for the appraised to identify features of the school's organization and management which inhibit effective performance or to offer suggestions for improvement. It is essential, also, that the appraiser should be aware of the numerous factors which directly affect appraisal. There are problems of bias which arise, for example, from age, sex, or ethnic origin and which may form an inevitable aspect of one individual's perception of another. The appraiser needs to develop empathy with those who are being appraised and avoid the possibility of one strongly positive or negative aspect of the appraisal directly influencing other factors.

The headteacher needs to link the appraisal of staff to staff development. Staff development has a major contribution to make to the effectiveness with which teachers and staff perform their jobs. In education the terms *training* and *development* have been used loosely. In general, the recent emphasis has been towards the concept of development, particularly in relation to whole-school development. There is a danger that this has been at the expense of the needs of individual teachers. Perhaps the term *training* has a more specific and sharper connotation which helps to re-establish that focus. Training should therefore be seen as a systematic development and improvement of the individual teacher's job performance which will enable the school to meet its goals. It should also enable the school to develop a bank of skills and knowledge which encourage it to be innovative and responsive to changing educational needs.

In general therefore the training of staff within the school develops through three major phases: initial training, induction, and in-service training. While schools are increasingly involved as partners in the initial training phase, the direct responsibility of the headteacher commences with an induction phase during which the employee is made more fully aware of the job context and the organization, and is given specific help and encouragement in a continuing learning process under the guidance of a teacher tutor. Induction complements the selection process. There follows a further developmental phase of in-service training. The important task faced by the headteacher is both an estimation of the future needs of the school and equipping the individual teacher to take his or her place in the general development of the school. Linked to this phase of training is training for specific tasks. New courses may be designed, new initiatives developed, all of which raise potential training issues.

The headteacher, as manager of the organization, must accept accountability for overall training. This may involve targeting training priorities and making time and resources available for training. It must be recognized that training requires investment. The headteacher must set the standards for such investment and attempt to measure its effectiveness. Local management of schools suggests that, in addition to school-based and school-focused staff development, there may be a need for specific, off-the-job training in newly required skills.

Leaving the organization

People leave the school voluntarily or as a result of dismissal, redundancy, redeployment, retirement, or death. Whenever staff are dismissed, the headteacher becomes directly involved in the application of the dismissal procedure. As stressed earlier, this will require the headteacher to collate and submit evidence to the governing body of the school. It therefore follows that the headteacher should monitor staff behaviour, and should be fully aware of the procedures relating to dismissal. The headteacher must develop a sense of judgement about the reasonableness of staff behaviour. This section will deal principally with the issues of redundancy and redeployment.

The scale of expenditure cuts by government inevitably raises the issue of substantial voluntary redundancies in education and compulsory redundancy in all parts of the education sector. From 1979–81 manual workers employed by local authorities decreased by 14 per cent. Teaching staff employed by local authorities declined by 4 per cent. There has been a particular impact upon part-time female employment, not simply in teaching but in the school meals and ancillary manual services sector.

The policy of open enrolment could result in the random, unplanned closure of schools, with little protection for displaced teachers. In such situations 'no redundancy' agreements may disappear and locally finance-managed schools in the same area will be under no obligation to accept redeployed teachers. Open enrolment therefore could result in some schools having falling pupil numbers which in turn could result in schools being required to lose staff. Governors of schools operating under local finance management schemes may decide for themselves pupil–teacher ratios and thus the number of teachers required.

Employees dismissed because of redundancy will be in a position to claim unfair dismissal if the reason for their selection was union membership or a breach of customary arrangements or an existing procedure. The situation may arise therefore where the headteacher, in conjunction with the governors, may be required to draw up a redundancy procedure, where formerly the responsibility lay with the LEA. In order to ensure a fair selection for redundancy, the headteacher should consider the need for a procedure which has reasonable or agreed criteria for selection. Such criteria may be service in the department, skill, conduct or performance. It may involve the maxim of 'last in, first out' which has been used in education although strong arguments have been made for curriculum-led staffing. Whatever criteria are adopted, there is a clear need for consistency of application and a recognized period of consultation.

There similarly exist in many local authorities agreements on selection for redeployment. Such agreements usually allow for maximum consultation and a voluntary process of redeployment. The criteria for selection usually include the needs of the school for particular expertise and subject specialisms. Local management of schools may restrict opportunities for redeployment.

Conclusion

This chapter described some of the staff management implications of running a school. The intention has not been to promote an exhaustive list of skills and techniques which would itself run to a textbook, but rather to highlight general areas of concern for schools. The chapter has attempted to place these implications into the context of the school, its organization, and environment. The educational environment over recent years has not been conducive to innovation or to development of co-operative staff relations. The recent legislation compounds these difficulties by directly imposing a challenging new range of responsibilities upon school management.

Problems of control and delegation, communication and discipline are clearly common to many types of complex organization. However, it is important to remember that schools have not been market-oriented institutions and that the primary tasks of schools are educational. Thus although there is much to be gained by a skilled approach to the issues of staff management, it must be remembered that headteachers derive their authority principally from their professional skill in managing the education of pupils. It is these skills of communication and organization, tolerance and understanding, which provide the headteacher with a considerable initial expertise.

Further Reading

Brewster, C. (1984) *Understanding Industrial Relations*, London: Pan Books.

Hawkins, K. (1979) *A Handbook of Industrial Relations Practice*, London: Kogan Page

March, J.G. (1974) 'Analytical skills: The university training of educational administrators', *Journal of Educational Administration*, vol. 12, no. 1.

Nicholls, A. (1983) *Managing Educational Innovations*, London: Routledge Kegan & Paul.

Palmer, G. (1983) *British Industrial Relations*, London: Allen & Unwin.

Peters, R.S. (1976) *The Role of the Head*, London: Routledge Kegan & Paul.

Ream, B. (1984) *Personnel Administration*, Cambridge: ICSA Publishing.

Tyson, S. and York, A. (1982) *Personnel Management Made Simple*, London: Heinemann.

Reid, I. (1978) *Sociological Perspectives on School and Education*, Wells Somerset: Open Books.

Chapter eight

The management of time

Cyril Wilkinson

The argument in the preceding chapters has been that, while headteachers are not required to become experts in accountancy, marketing, law and so on, the range of their responsibilities, nevertheless, has widened. If senior staff are to continue to exercise academic leadership in addition to these new responsibilities then the management of time becomes a crucial issue on their agenda. The limitation of a finite amount of time is identified by many headteachers as one of the most serious constraints they face in attempting to meet the challenges presented by the changed managerial arena.

Images have been used to attempt to capture the nature of time. It has been presented as a commodity with a currency value which may vary in exchange rate according to social, geographic, or market forces. In some cultures one is made to feel guilty if time is 'wasted' while in others time is regarded more casually. Benjamin Franklin (1745) took the imagery a stage further when he counselled 'Remember that time is money': time is certainly now accounted in terms of sums of money per hour, per week, per month, and per year. The increasing use in education of techniques like cost–benefit analysis implies a hardheaded accounting of the cost elements in time. The delegation of financial management to school level will require those who have managerial responsibility to engage in this kind of accounting exercise. Managers in schools are often surprised to discover that a staff meeting of fifty members of staff for three hours at a nominal eight pounds per hour for each participant costs one thousand two hundred pounds. This puts a premium on the worthwhile utilization of time.

Time may also be seen as the composite total of that available to and utilized by all the staff in the school. The stipulation under the School Teachers' Pay and Conditions Order (DES 1987) of a minimum of 1,265 hours has made teachers particularly sensitive to the extent of their obligation in terms of time. Headteachers, therefore, have had to look at the total deployment of staff time and to agree with individual members of staff how their time is to be used. Clear job specifications for staff, negotiated through sympathetic and reciprocal processes of appraisal which relate to the aims and objectives of the school and the priorities identified, can be useful instruments in achieving more effective utilization of the total bank of time available. However, the dangers of teachers' contracts which are tightly defined may be seen in many American schools where principals find it impossible to hold meetings after school hours or to persuade staff to engage in extra-curricular activities. This chill wind is already being felt in the United Kingdom and can only be avoided by the establishment of sensitive relationships which allow flexibility.

In many of the devolved activities of LMS there will be a need for effective staff development if delegated tasks and functions are to be undertaken successfully. Such initiatives will demand valuable time and sympathetic provision by LEAs. For example, in many primary schools where curriculum development has been growing in volume and more closely associated with the new allowance structures, staff have been relating uneasily to unfamiliar roles. In such times of significant change and insecurity LEAs must be generous in providing opportunity for development and regeneration. It is important to build solid foundations for future evolution. Advisory and consultancy services working in partnership with institutions of higher education can offer invaluable support and guidance in the implementation of LMS. Schools can also look at different sources of provision and buy appropriately, having made a searching diagnosis of needs and priorities. Educational institutions will have to learn, like many successful private sector organizations, that ongoing staff development is of key importance and costs money and time.

More responsibilities deriving from the new activities devolved on schools will demand more time. Local financial management is a key example. Decision-making structures will be required to determine financial priorities before arriving at the activities of budgeting and accounting. There has been a movement towards more participation in decision making at middle-management level and below but such democratic involvement consumes time. However, it need not be time taken up wholly in meetings. Staff can be encouraged to submit ideas and proposals in written form which may be considered by senior management and the problematic areas addressed specifically.

The other side of the coin is the removal of layers of intermediate administration which inhibit the school's ability to act swiftly. In the past schools wishing to purchase items of equipment had to approach a purchasing officer in the LEA who followed a lengthy procedure of obtaining estimates and choosing an appropriate provider. While the headteacher is accountable to the school governors for good house-keeping and must spend wisely, it will now be possible to expedite purchase. Admission of pupils to schools, which is considered in the second chapter of the 1988 Act, offers another example of time saving to hard-pressed management. A standard number for each school is determined in most cases by the number of pupils admitted in 1979 or in schools established since then by the number fixed when they came into being. No longer will schools have to await the LEA decision on admission numbers arrived at (on occasion) in arbitrary fashion and often too late for effective decision making. Open enrolment may be threatening to many schools but it will certainly save time.

Identifying priorities

Approaches to more effective management of time have often taken as a starting point the compilation of a diary chronicling how time is utilized at present. This approach is predicated on a belief prevalent in management literature that it is important to know where you are now before determining where you want to go. The problem with this method of attack is the difficulty in designing an analytic instrument which makes sense of the myriad of data obtained. The result is that many investigations such as that undertaken by Hall, Mackay, and Morgan (1986) simply reflect what headteachers in schools already know – that their working day is hectic and fragmented and their activity characterized by brevity and variety. The approach proposed here is to identify priorities in the use of time as a first step so that the process of analysis and evaluation which follows is more clearly focused within an appropriate framework.

The establishment of priorities and goals is a key activity for the effective education manager otherwise he is likely to be blown by whatever wind is strongest. In the nebulous world of education, where ends and means are questioned and disputed, the lack of clarity is often compounded by the manager who takes on everything that is asked of him and is unwilling to say 'No'. The setting of priorities is about deciding what is important and the following priorities profile is offered as an aid to such investigation.

Priorities profile

- *What are your long-term aspirations for the school?* A common problem claimed by staff in schools is that it is difficult to identify and sustain a clear sense of mission. The vision of the way forward becomes lost in the clinging mud of day-to-day problems and emergencies.
- *What do you identify as your role in pursuing these aspirations?* It is important that senior management takes a

helicopter view so that the urgent and pressing but less important does not force out consideration of important objectives both in the short-term and long-term. The headteacher, in particular, has a central responsibility to keep the main objectives of the school in sight.

- *What do you see as your major management priorities?* Kotter (1982) maintains that it is crucial for the manager to have a clear 'agenda' with established priorities. He argues that, although the manager's world is frenetic, spasmodic, and often reactive, it is, nevertheless, purposive. For example, a deputy headteacher with responsibility for staff development may determine needs and exercise influence through the informal networks. The daily encounters with colleagues may provide opportunities to share and explore issues of concern both for the individual and the school.
- *What are the main management activities involved in pursuing these priorities?* The main argument in the preceding chapters is that it is important for senior staff to identify the main management tasks and to decide which to retain and which to delegate. The headteachers have considerable flexibility in determining what their major contributions are to be but must ensure that the various functions are clearly assigned. The headteacher retains ultimate accountability and the functions newly devolved to school level must be included among the priorities.

By a carefully planned and clearly articulated process of delegation senior staff can have a more certain picture of the specific activities each wishes or is required to be engaged in. For example, within the new framework of the national curriculum a senior teacher may have curriculum design as a high priority. It will be necessary to look beyond the 'global curriculum' and to identify key areas for attention. Such areas may be determined by the core and foundation subjects of the proposed national curriculum or it may be expedient to respond to growing and newly developing areas like economic awareness, health education, and information technology. In both cases it is necessary to decide the nature of the support to be given, the action required and the demands on energy and time.

Primary schools will have particular difficulty in finding time for curriculum development and in addressing the many activities associated with LMS. As primary teachers tend to relate to one class or grouping for most of the working day it is not easy to find cover to release staff. This is also particularly true of the teaching principal in smaller schools. Some schools have met this challenge by adopting pedagogical approaches like team teaching and resource-based learning. Other primary schools have formed cluster groups or consortia to allow exchange of staff and, in some cases, an extra member of staff has been negotiated with the LEA to manufacture free time and to obtain specialist curriculum expertise. The challenge is to look closely and critically at prevailing practice and to devise ways of making time available.

Present use of time

The following questions should assist the manager to compile a more complete picture of present management activities and to compare these with the desired activities identified through the use of the priorities profile paying particular attention to the new demands imposed by the 1988 Act.

1 What are the main management activities in which you engage at present?
2 How are these activities determined? (job description, prescription from above, negotiation, established practice, self-determination.)
3 Are these the activities identified as your priorities?
4 How much time do you give to important and less-important tasks as you see them?
5 How much time do you spend on activities which you feel do not benefit pupils, staff, the school or yourself? On whom/what is this time spent?

A searching, rigorous response to the above questions requires some kind of methodical investigation of present practice. The priorities identified and ordered earlier and the nature of the specific questions to which an answer is desired will determine the choice of approach used to ascertain how time is currently spent. It is desirable for the individual to design a specific instrument on the basis of the priorities identified. Too often instruments are designed without a clear perception of the exact information that is required and in what form it is wanted.

Figure 8.1 offers a simple four quadrant framework which may be used to locate and analyse the spectrum of management activity recorded in the time log. It is likely that most managers operate in quadrants 1 and 2 and are therefore working under constant stress and pressure. Often they may not be initiating events but are merely reacting to demands from others. Perhaps they are unwilling to say 'No' and therefore are doing many of the tasks which should be done by colleagues. There may be a lack of clarity about role and functions in the school so that unexpected problems are more likely to surface. Quadrant 2 is perhaps the most uncomfortable and least satisfying in which to reside although some managers may be happy to feel busy engaging in trivial pursuits. A manager in Quadrant 3 is more likely to be undertaking important tasks and addressing key problems in circumstances over which he has control and influence. Hopefully the message is clear – routine and trivial administrative tasks and crisis action are categories of activity that should be reduced and replaced as far as possible by the important, whether immediate or long-term. Perhaps one of the positive outcomes of the new Act will be to encourage schools and their governing bodies to engage in more proactive long-term activities and in this context the issue of strategic planning addressed later in this chapter is of particular importance.

Figure 8.1 Classification framework

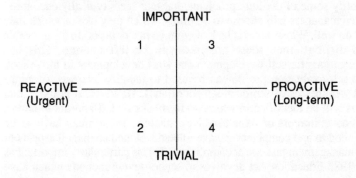

IMPORTANT

1   3

REACTIVE ———————————|——————————— PROACTIVE
(Urgent)   (Long-term)

2   4

TRIVIAL

Self-evaluation

The scrutiny of how time is utilized leads inevitably to scrutiny of self. It is only by knowing ourselves better that many of the difficulties and resolutions may be identified. Often we are inclined to step back and refuse to acknowledge certain aspects of our personality which pose problems. Appropriate excuses are often made: 'I always work best under pressure'; 'I cannot respond until I have the necessary information to hand'; 'If colleagues have problems I cannot refuse to see them'; 'It will not be done if I do not do it myself'. An honest response to the following self-evaluation profile will provide helpful indicators of temperament and disposition, strengths and weaknesses. It also asks about activity which is not work related but makes an important contribution to a more complete, balanced, and fulfilled life.

Self-evaluation profile

- Which management activities do you do best?
- Which management activities do you dislike doing?
- When and in what circumstances do you feel under time pressure?
- Do you feel that you succeed in balancing work-based activities and your private life? If not, which areas are neglected?
- Do you feel that generally you have energy and dynamism to spare?
- Do you manage to build free time into your working day?
- If you could remodel your job what changes would you make?
- If you could reorder your allocation of time what changes would you make?

The answers to the above questions should increase self-awareness and identify some of the time problems that managers typically encounter. Often managers will choose to do things which they like or which they can do well. Where there is lack of competence or tasks are disagreeable and difficult then these are likely to be left undone. This has implications for self-development and staff development in the school. The self-evaluation profile can be used to identify interests, strengths and weaknesses of senior members of staff. However, it is likely that areas will be identified in which no member of staff appears to have a particular interest or expertise. Nevertheless, these areas have to be attended to and competences have to be developed so that all aspects of the management task are accomplished. This is particularly important as the 1988 Education Act devolves to school level functions which have not been located there traditionally. As stated earlier the headteacher does not have to become an accountant but often expertise does reside at a senior level within the school. Ideally there is a case for an ancillary addition to establishment with expertise and seniority.

Research into educational institutions (Martin and Willower 1981) has indicated that early morning is often the busiest time - telephone calls, correspondence, unresolved problems from the previous day are typical pressures on the manager. Schools are also characterized by cyclical activity. Budgeting, requisitioning, timetabling, and the preparing of reports and profiles are characteristic examples and may be alleviated by appropriate delegation and dispersion. It is likely that the reader can identify colleagues who are 'workaholics'. Typically they work long hours and bring reams of paper home. Family, friends and leisure suffer at the expense of work. Adair (1988) points out that the Pareto principle also applies to time – 80 per cent of the really productive, creative work will be done in 20 per cent of the time. Allocation of appropriate time to home, family, relaxation, and recreation will lead to a happier, more fulfilled, balanced life style and reduce the likelihood of stress-related illnesses. Research has indicated that managerial activity is often fragmented, unremitting, and spontaneous. Much of this piecemeal, disjointed behaviour may be positive and purposive but equally much may occur because of lack of organization and the assumption of an unthinking management style.

Obstacles to effective time management

The last two questions in the evaluation profile ask managers to look critically at their present activity and allocation of time and to devise ways in which both may be revised to increase effectiveness. Such diagnosis may be helped by the identification of recurring problems in managing time which may be tackled and overcome.

Procrastination

To defer or put off action until some future time without reasonable justification is a very human failing. Compelling reasons may be sought and produced: 'I'm too busy now to respond to that problem – I'll look at it again when I have more time' or 'Allow the dust to settle'. It may be on occasion that deferment is a sound course of action but if it happens habitually then its validity must be questioned. Often unpleasant or demanding tasks are put off which become more difficult with each succeeding day. In addition, work piles up and important information may be buried with it leading to missed deadlines. If it has become habitual to be dilatory then one must determine to break the pattern. Often it is a case of taking a simple, first step – that meeting with the awkward member of staff or breaking of unwelcome news – which often turns out to be less threatening than was imagined. It is perhaps more difficult to change behaviour which reflects a casual and easy-going personality. The setting of personal deadlines and adhering to them offers one way of establishing order and priority. It is salutary to remember that tomorrow never comes and the temptation to defer should be resisted.

Open door

'Open door' became a fashionable management maxim in the 1960s. It suggested management which was accessible, responsive and sympathetic but for many managers the other side of the coin was a plethora of often unwelcome interruptions. Clearly it is important to offer ready access to staff, parents, or other parties if the need arises and in such circumstances interruptions may be inevitable. However there are valid and invalid interruptions, and judgements have to be made to decide the validity of claims on time. There are a number of filters which may be employed. If structures and channels of communication are clearly delineated the caller may be referred to the pertinent member of staff. Very often headteachers and senior managers have a secretary or access to one who can defer callers, keep them at bay or pass them to the appropriate colleague. This has implications for effective delegation which will be considered later. When the enforced interruptions are inevitable there are strategies which may be employed to abbreviate them:

- Identify the purpose of the visit and stick to it.
- Set apart times of the day for open access.
- Limit the time for each caller and specify it.
- Body language is important: do not become comfortably seated and established.

Task jumping

Often the most frequent source of interruption is the manager himself. If a task becomes difficult then one is tempted to turn to something else. Many find it difficult to concentrate for protracted periods of time. It is prudent to remember that more is likely to be achieved in one hour of continuous application than in several hours of interrupted work because a recovery period is necessary after each stoppage. It is expedient to discover if the task jumping is self-inflicted. Mintzberg (1973) found that five chief executives under investigation 'frequently interrupted their desk work to place telephone calls or to request that subordinates come by'. Martin and Willower (1981) in their investigation of the managerial behaviour of five high-school principals found that most (81.4 per cent) of the activities that the subjects entered into ranged from one to four minutes and the modal time duration for the 3,730 tasks observed over 25 days was one minute. Also 50 per cent of all observed activities were interrupted. They call this pattern of behaviour 'The busy person syndrome'. Perhaps the sheer volume of work may offer some explanation but it would also appear that the managers contributed in part to the problem. Effort is required to break the frenetic cycle of activity and to build in some more coherent pattern of work.

Administrivia

In management terminology a distinction is often made in the United Kingdom between management and administration. Administration is portrayed as the mechanical, routine support and maintenance of a system with administrators frequently lacking the authority to make judgements and decisions in key areas like policy making and the allocation of resources. On the other hand, management involves crucial processes like problem solving, planning, decision making, organizing, leading, and influencing. The term 'administrivia' has a further connotation implying engagement in trivialities and unimportant detail. Hall, MacKay, and Morgan (1986) in their study of fifteen headteachers demonstrated that some devoted considerable time to such activity and it is certainly a common complaint by headteachers that 'administrivia' so often take over. There are clear implications for judicious delegation and the sharing out of routine matters to allow senior management to address important matters of policy and its implementation.

Meetings

Hall, Mackay, and Morgan (1986) also discovered that an overwhelming volume of headteachers' activity was interpersonal. While many of the interchanges were with individuals, a considerable amount of time was taken up with meetings. A meeting may be described as the organized or spontaneous coming together of people at a common time and place for specific purposes. These purposes may be predetermined or may arise from a chance encounter with a group of colleagues. Because meetings may take up and waste substantial amounts of time headteachers have to consider them critically. They may decide to carry out a review of meetings in the school and, in particular, those which they attend. Relevant questions may include:

- Are the meetings (series of meetings) necessary?
- If they are necessary what is their purpose?
- How often do they take place?
- How many meetings are required?
- Do I need to attend? If the answer is 'yes', do I need to attend all of them?

There is no doubt that meetings contribute vitally to the effective management of a school but it is to be suspected that many unnecessary meetings are held when the group has already fulfilled its function or when intervening activity or time for reflection is required. Meetings may serve a variety of purposes including the following:

- Information giving/exchange
- Direction
- Problem solving

- Discussion
- Negotiation
- Decision-making

It may well be that many of these activities occur in the course of a meeting but it is helpful for the manager to have a clear, predominant purpose in his mind. For example, given the new curriculum specification emerging from the 1988 Education Act it may be appropriate to hold a preliminary meeting to discuss what the implications are for the school but definitive decision making may be deferred to a later meeting to allow all parties to reflect upon and propose possible courses of action. Because meetings are costly as illustrated earlier, the manager may decide to be ruthless in his review.

However, in a dynamic school meetings are important instruments which encourage commitment and participation and if they are necessary then there are ways of saving time. It may be appropriate to delegate functions to smaller groups who report back either to senior management, larger groupings, or full staff meetings. It is worthwhile to prepare carefully and to provide preliminary documentation which may be digested before rather than during the meeting. If possible formal meetings should not be called at short notice. Agenda should be brief and adhered to.

The chairperson occupies a key position in acting both as leader and adjudicator. The chairperson can decide in advance what is the maximum time for each item and, if necessary, operate a guillotine. The tone of the meeting may be set by a clear exposition of the purpose of the meeting and by demonstrating conciseness and clarity throughout. It is sound practice not to allow decisions arrived at in previous meetings to be reconsidered and reversed unless there are serious reasons for so doing. The chairperson can discourage the discursive, dominant, and dilatory and be firm, fair and supportive without being dismissive. The momentum should be sustained without losing healthy, pertinent discussion and the generation of ideas.

Strategies for more effective time management

Having identified some of the problems which may contribute to time pressure for those who manage schools some strategies for recovery, if not total cure, emerge from the process of diagnosis.

Planning and the setting of goals

Many experts who have pronounced and written on management, stress the importance of setting goals or intentions for the organization and by implication for those who work within it (Bolman and Deal 1984). This projection of targets, a looking and thinking forward in time, is central to the process of planning. While recognizing the political and transitory reality of schools it is nevertheless possible by careful, proactive planning to make more effective use of time. The term 'goal' clearly derives from sporting endeavours and is the declared intention of teams of players. There is the implication that all team members are or should be co-operating and contributing to that end. Such a claim should not be taken for granted in organizations like schools where territory and competition are central to the culture and value systems, and may stimulate behaviour which does not seek to pursue common aims. Equally status, reward, autonomy, professional interest and individual fulfilment are personal goals which may not be in harmony with the goals of those who manage and therefore seek the general good of the school.

A second series of analogies comes from the military world. Strategy and tactics are concepts which are often used in referring to the planning process. Wilkinson and Cave (1987) present a framework, shown in Figure 8.2, which offers a three-fold hierarchy of specificity.

Figure 8.2 A framework for planning

Dimensions of planning		
Specificity	*Level*	*Time scale*
Strategic	School wide	Long-term
Tactical	School years	Medium-term
Operational	Class	Short -term

Strategic planning is about establishing more long-term intentions for the school and the determination of overall policy. It was suggested earlier that strategic planning will be required to meet the many activities involved in the local management of schools. The term 'strategy' derives from a Greek word meaning 'command of a general' and therefore implies that senior management will have a key role to play although it will be ultimately sanctioned by the headteacher and governing body who carry overall responsibility for the school.

Five- and indeed ten-year plans have become common practice in private- and public-sector organizations including education. Because tightly defined goals and objectives may prescribe the activity and therefore limit the flexibility and responsiveness of organizations the concept of rolling plans has emerged which implies frequent review and revision of goals and objectives. In key areas like curriculum development this may mean weekly or monthly monitoring of progress and direction. The range of application from the total school to the individual classroom stresses the importance of co-ordinated communication and decision-making structures. In time span tactical planning refers to the medium term and may particularly involve middle management like heads of department or subject co-ordinators who may concentrate on annual programmes and the way forward over the following two or three years. It is important that they should be aware of the longer-term canvas and make allowance for it. Operational planning refers to the short term and therefore in schools the primary focus will be the classroom and the more immediate concerns of the practising teacher typified by lesson plans. The integration of planning and time dimensions should ensure a more coherent specification and implementation of goals and objectives and therefore less likelihood of a rudderless ship which loses valuable time in deviations from course.

Figure 8.3 presents a model of planning which may be applied to schools and identifies key external and internal participants and sources of influence. The activities of review and audit seek to offer a more complete picture of the working environment. Review reminds us that knowing where we have been (the past) and where we are (the present) are vital contributions to determining where we want to go (the future). The activity of audit identifies what opportunities and threats are facing the school and what are strengths and weaknesses. This exercise reminds us that managing is the art of the possible and the process of audit is about deciding what is possible.

Mission has become a popular term in planning parlance and refers to the overall aspirations of the school. The mission statement may be regarded as the foundation stone of school purposes and policy. The terms 'aim' and 'goal' are often used interchangeably and express in general terms intentions which the school seeks to pursue. Targets and objectives are usually more specific declarations of intent often expressed in behavioural terms. It is sound practice to make aims, goals, and objectives as specific and realistic as possible and to ensure that they are attainable but demanding. It is also expedient to set reasonable deadlines which may be modified if circumstances change. By judicious management of time the headteacher can ensure that (s)he is properly engaged in the development of strategies and tactics rather than becoming totally enmeshed in short-term operations.

Delegation

There is, in a typical school, an often untapped bank of expertise and knowledge available from both staff and pupils. Frequently senior managers are tempted to undertake tasks which can be carried out very competently by others. The delegation of such tasks should free the

Figure 8.3 The planning process

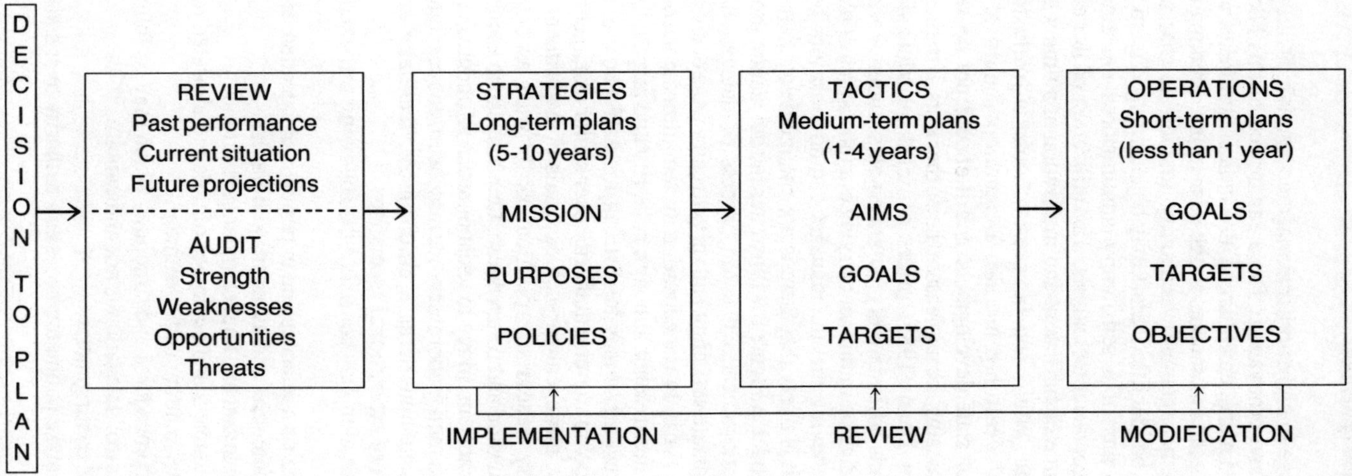

DECISION TO PLAN

REVIEW	STRATEGIES	TACTICS	OPERATIONS
Past performance	Long-term plans	Medium-term plans	Short-term plans
Current situation	(5-10 years)	(1-4 years)	(less than 1 year)
Future projections			
	MISSION	AIMS	GOALS
AUDIT	PURPOSES	GOALS	TARGETS
Strength	POLICIES	TARGETS	OBJECTIVES
Weaknesses			
Opportunities			
Threats			

IMPLEMENTATION   REVIEW   MODIFICATION

manager to engage in higher order management activities like planning, policy making, and innovating. The areas treated in this book arising from the changed management arena also indicate priorities which will be high on the agenda of schools in the near future. Banking offers the term 'audit' to management vocabulary to indicate that talent and competence can be identified. Staff may be encouraged to specify their strengths by means of a sensitively administered questionnaire or through skilful appraisal techniques. The utilization of those strengths offers a rich source of fulfilment and motivation at a time when a lack of mobility both within and between schools is likely to lead to debilitation and declining morale. Delegation should also be an important tool of staff development and it should not be seen as an opportunity for passing the unpleasant, boring aspects of management to other staff. Joan Dean (1985) offers a useful questionnaire: if the manager responds affirmatively to statements about working long hours, concentrating on minutiae, carrying out jobs which could be done by others and believing that the manager can do most jobs better than colleagues then it is likely that there is not enough delegation.

The simple model in Figure 8.4 illustrates the delegation process. The principle of parity indicates that the process of delegation involves giving the subordinate sufficient authority to carry out a decision as well as responsibility for it. In the education system ultimate accountability resides with the headteacher although authority and responsibility may be delegated. However, it may be difficult for staff who are relatively junior in the school to exercise authority over senior management or, on occasion, middle management such as heads of department and year heads. This may necessitate political skills such as negotiation, bargaining, persuasion and compromise. One has also to remember that professional teachers are likely to resist bureaucratic control as typified in the terms 'boss' and 'subordinate'. It may be more acceptable for the superior to present himself as a co-ordinator, facilitator or enabler managing a team of professional specialists.

Effective delegation may consist of the following activities:

- Find out the competences and experience of intended delegates.
- Introduce intention and ascertain willingness.
- Organize relevant staff development activity.
- Define parameters and outcomes of task and allocated resources.
- Check understanding and agreement.
- Determine procedures and structures which may be followed if problems arise: delegation is not abdication.
- Provide for contingencies.
- Grant and make public the necessary authority over staff and resources.

- Offer feedback and positive reinforcement where appropriate.
- Carry out regular review unobtrusively.

Figure 8.4 The process of delegation

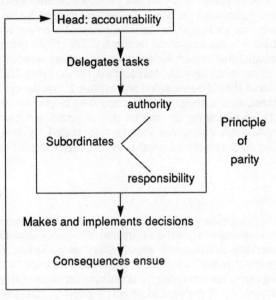

Peak time

There are differences between individuals in relation to when they work best. Some maintain that they work most effectively late at night while others prefer to rise early and use the first hours of the morning. Physiologists claim that the human metabolism is governed by biorhythms or cycles which are reinforced by the imposed periods of sleep and waking. This would suggest that people should be fresher and more energetic in the morning after a good night's rest. Given that the human body also burns energy through the course of a hard working day it is likely that teachers who have worked hard from early morning to the end of the school day may find it difficult to regenerate themselves to reasonable levels of efficiency in the evening. The argument to date supports the validity of testing one's capacity to work in the early morning if this has not been tried before or at least to use the morning hours in preference to afternoon or evening. Research also indicates that people work better if there are breaks to allow the system to revitalize itself. The number and timing of breaks may be determined by the nature of the task being undertaken. Creative work demands freshness and dynamism while routine administration may be less demanding. Nevertheless, repetitive work also demands concentration if mistakes are to be avoided.

Psychologists claim that the mind works even during sleep and in the process of sleeping on a problem the subconscious mind may offer a solution. Apart from the possibility of new insights it also makes sense to 'sleep' on an important decision to avoid arriving at unwarranted conclusions in the heat of the moment. Adair (1988) offers the concept of 'moonlighting' which he describes as waking naturally in the early hours of the morning with ideas tumbling in the mind. He suggests that those ideas should be recorded and captured. The danger of saturation and exhaustion through working too long supports the wisdom of suitably apportioning the school day if protracted concentration is required. Such endeavour can be punctuated by less demanding activities such as more informal conversations with staff or visitors.

Free time

Long working hours, excessive paper work, the pressure of deadlines, frequent interruptions, and the intrusion of the unexpected all contribute to a working environment which offers no opportunity to recharge batteries or to pause for reflection and critical review of what the school is doing and where it is going. Unremitting pressure of work is likely to lead to stress and the myriad of accompanying symptoms which are often recognized only at crisis point. Perhaps the increasing inclusion of consideration of stress in conference sessions and the growing volume of research into its causes and remedies are indications of a growing recognition of pressures in schools, not least the pressure of time. If the manager can set apart a period of time each day for quiet reflection and consideration of what tomorrow and the longer term future may bring, it is more probable that he can remain in control of the management environment. The time log mentioned earlier offers an instrument to review critically what is being done. The manager can ask himself two questions: 'Is this activity necessary?', and 'What would happen if I did not do it?' Delegation and the reduction of time spent in attending meetings and routine administration may offer the opportunity to do less a little better and to make that small but vital oasis of free time for regeneration and relaxation. Colleagues and secretaries may be conditioned to respect and protect it and the location of the daily half an hour may alter from day to day to accommodate the changing pattern of management practice.

Conclusion

This chapter has concentrated on the identification and setting of priorities as a framework for effective management of time. It therefore would seem appropriate to distil what has gone before and to identify some guidelines to assist managers in educational institutions to use their time better.

- Identify long-term, middle-term, and short-term goals/targets for the school and yourself.
- Determine the important and less important tasks and allocate time accordingly.
- Engage in frank self-analysis to discover strengths and weaknesses.
- Increase proactivity and reduce reactivity where it is possible.
- Review utilization of time periodically (termly, six-monthly).
- Delegate effectively.
- Look critically at the management of meetings and individual encounters.
- Use peak time and build in periods of free time.
- Balance work and private life.
- Set reasonable deadlines and reduce procrastination.
- Learn to say 'No'.
- Plan your programme of activity daily, weekly, termly, and annually and try to stick to it without threatening responsiveness and flexibility.

It may be expedient to remember Murphy's Law which offers wise advice not merely about time but about the complex world of management:

> 'Nothing is as easy as it looks.
> Everything takes longer than you expect.
> And if anything can go wrong it will
> At the worst possible moment.'

References

Adair, J. (1988) *Effective Time Management*, London: Pan.
Bolman, L.G. and Deal, T.E. (1984) *Modern Approaches to Understanding and Managing Organisations*, San Francisco: Jossey Bass.
Dean, J. (1985), *Managing the Secondary School*, London: Croom Helm.

DES (1987) *School Teachers' Pay and Conditions*, London: HMSO.

Franklin, B. (1745) *Advice to a Young Tradesman*, Philadelphia: Humphreys.

Hall, V., MacKay, H., and Morgan, C. (1986) *Head Teachers at Work*, Milton Keynes: Open University Press.

Kotter, J.P. (1982) *The General Manager*, London: Free Press.

Martin, W.J. and Willower, D.J. (1981) 'The managerial behavior of High School Principals', *Educational Administration Quarterly*, vol. 17, no. 1.

Mintzberg, H. (1973) *The Nature of Managerial Work*, London: Harper & Row.

Wilkinson, C. and Cave, E. (1987) *Teaching and Managing: Inseparable Activities in Schools*, London: Croom Helm.

Further reading

Drucker, P. (1967) *The Effective Executive*, London: Heinemann.

Oncken, W. (1984) *Managing Management Time*, New York: Prentice Hall.

Pedler, M., Burgoyne, J. and Boydell, T. (1978) *A Manager's Guide to Self Development*, New York: McGraw Hill.

Index